The Real World War

The Real World War

THE COMING BATTLE FOR

AND WHY

THE NEW GLOBAL ECONOMY
WE ARE IN DANGER OF LOSING

Hunter Lewis & Donald Allison

Coward, McCann & Geoghegan
NEW YORK

The authors gratefully acknowledge permission to quote from
the following material:
   "Consumer Reports Repair Records of 1980 Model Cars."
Copyright 1981 by Consumers Union of United States, Inc.,
Mount Vernon, NY 10550. Reprinted by permission from
Consumer Reports, April 1981.
   Four Quartets by T. S. Eliot. Copyright 1943 by T. S. Eliot;
copyright renewed 1971 by Esme Valerie Eliot. Reprinted by
permission of Harcourt Brace Jovanovich, Inc.

Library of Congress Cataloging in Publication Data

Lewis, Hunter.
   The real world war.

   Bibliography: p.
   Includes index.
   1. Technological innovations—United States.
2. Competition, International. I. Allison, Donald. II. Title.
HC110.T4L49   1982   337.73   81-19548
ISBN 0-698-11122-2   AACR2

Printed in the United States of America

Contents

The Real World War

Introduction

If there is a single great fact of our era, it is not the continuing rivalry between Russia and the West. Instead, it is the emergence of the first truly international industrial marketplace and the struggle between the leading trading nations and blocs—the United States, Western Europe, Japan, Singapore–Taiwan–Hong Kong–Korea, Mexico–Brazil, and, potentially, China—to control this new global economy.

In the crucial battle for this new world marketplace, the first round was inevitably won by the United States. In 1967, J. J. Servan-Schreiber, founder of the French weekly news magazine *L'Express,* published a book, *The American Challenge,* about the overwhelming economic power of the United States and the threat this power posed for Europe. In the introduction he wrote: "Starting with a rather matter-of-fact examination of American investment in Europe, we find an economic system that is in a state of collapse. It is our own. We see a foreign challenger breaking down the . . . framework of our societies. We are witnessing the prelude to our own historical bankruptcy. . . ."

But Servan-Schreiber's book proved to be less than prophetic. Contrary to everyone's expectations, the United States lost the second round of the battle for world markets to Japan, Western Europe, and the newly industrialized countries of Asia and South America. In 1971, the U.S. suffered its first trade deficit since 1935, its second in this century. Since then American companies have lost world leadership in one major international industry after another.

This process is relatively well known in the steel, auto, and consumer electronics industries. Philip Caldwell, president of Ford Motor Company, has warned that present trends could lead to the extinction of the automobile industry in North America.

What is even more alarming is that high-technology industries such as semiconductors, computers, and aerospace, which America has long dominated, are also under heavy attack. If the battle is lost in these and other emerging technologies, the United States will become, in the words of Thibaut de Saint Phalle, a former director of the American Export-Import Bank, "a developing country in ten or fifteen years."

These events are often confused with related but quite different problems. Any of several crises could bring down our economy: dependence on Middle Eastern energy; a domestic financial structure overloaded with consumer and corporate debt; an international financial structure unable to cope with billions of dollars of Third World and Eastern European debts that may never be repaid; a jerry-built international currency market; high inflation rates; and continuing high unemployment.

Yet these multiple crises, important and potentially lethal as they are, tend to mask an even more fundamental danger in our loss of world markets. Like visitors to Plato's famous cave, we are mesmerized by the shadows that dance on the walls and miss the underlying truth: we could win the latest cold war over the Middle East, restore our financial system, beat back inflation, recession, and unemployment and still slip away into economic and historical oblivion.

There is an important counterargument that it does not really matter. According to this view, the desire to control world markets is simply a manifestation of jingoism and greed. One need not, however, be jingoistic or greedy to wonder what values would prevail in a post-American world.

The Real World War addresses these issues, but is principally about the next round of the struggle for global economic dominance. If the book has an overriding theme, it is that time is growing short. Most people, even most businessmen and economists, think that an international market means an open-ended contest in which industry leadership constantly shifts between countries and companies. Japan may shine for a moment only to be supplanted by Korea–Hong Kong–Taiwan–Singapore, or the cycle may swing back to favor established competitors in North America or Europe. In this view of more or less constant change, there can be neither permanent winners nor permanent losers.

The reality, however, is fundamentally different. The truly international market that has finally evolved represents a finite opportunity. For several more decades at least, the current state of accelerated change—even of industrial chaos—will continue unabated as national economies strive to adjust to the new international order. Eventually, however, clear winners will emerge with gigantic shares of international production.

As the rate of change and growth slows, the cost of challenging these entrenched monoliths will inevitably rise and it will become increasingly difficult for newcomers to destabilize the system. Those countries and companies that understand what is happening and make the necessary sacrifices now will come to enjoy unparalleled and unimaginable wealth in the future. Those that fail for any reason—lack of understanding, resources, or determination—may find other, more limited opportunities in new technologies or products, but they will have missed the greater chance in the final transition from national economies to a single world market.

In the climactic battle for world market share that is now unfolding, no competitor enjoys greater natural advantages than the United States. We possess all the necessary resources. When pressed, we have always had the will. What we still lack is sufficient understanding. We have not only underestimated the urgency of the struggle, but have also failed to apply some of the most basic rules for success in a world economy. Ironically, these rules have been developed in a formal sense by American business consultants and academics—not by foreigners.

Over the past decade, a whole new body of American business theory has grown up. One single element—market share theory—represents the most important innovation in economics since the development of Keynesianism during the Great Depression. Yet, inexplicably, we have not made full use of the new and powerful tools at our disposal.

Will the United States recover from fifteen years of drift and inertia to win the third and perhaps final round in the battle for world markets? The answer—the only possible answer—is the one that we make for ourselves.

Part One

The Battle for
Industrial Supremacy

1 The American Collapse

American industrial power is in precipitous decline. Wherever one looks, the evidence is inescapable:

• In 1965, our largest industrial company, General Motors, earned *twice* as much as the combined total of the thirty largest German industrial companies *and* the thirty largest Japanese industrial companies. In 1980, GM reported its first loss since the Great Depression.

• In 1965, American industrial companies with sales of over $1 billion represented 70 percent of all such companies in the world. By 1980, our share had fallen to 40 percent:

1965 Sales Over $1 Billion	*Number*
United States	60
European Economic Community*	24
Other Western Nations	1
Japan	2
Developing Countries	0

1981 Sales Over $1 Billion	*Number*
United States	301
European Economic Community	206
Other Western Nations	110
Japan	103
Developing Countries	35

*Members include Belgium, Denmark, France, Greece, Ireland, Italy, The Netherlands, Luxembourg, The United Kingdom, and West Germany.

• Since the mid-sixties, American companies have been devastated in many of the basic industries that propelled our economic growth after World War Two. Our share of the world consumer electronics market (radios, TVs, etc.) has fallen from 35 to 10 percent; of the world steel market from 26 to 17 percent; and of the world automobile market from 44 to 25 percent.

Even worse, we have lost ground in the high-technology industries that were once virtually an American monopoly. Our share of the total world market for wide-bodied jets has fallen from approximately 95 to 65 percent. In the crucial area of semiconductors, we have fallen from 90 to 60 percent of the world market.

• The same sickness that is evident at the company and industry level also reveals itself at the national level. In 1970, American gross national product, the value of all goods and services produced in our economy, represented 30 percent of total world gross national product. By the end of the decade, our share had fallen to just over 20 percent. Even Italy, with few natural resources and a troubled political system, grew faster than the United States in real terms (after adjusting for inflation) throughout the 1970s. Japan grew twice as fast while newly industrialized countries (NICs) in the Pacific Basin soared off the charts. Besides the United States, only the Soviet Union lost relative world-market share. Every other major country or trading bloc gained ground.

• As America's share of world GNP has declined, so has our share of world export trade. Between 1965 and 1980, world trade exploded from $150 billion to $1.5 trillion per year. Our own exports failed to keep pace, falling from 17.3 percent to 12.9 percent of the world total. As a result, our trade balance plummeted from a $5.4 billion surplus to a $37 billion deficit during this period.*

*Oil imports are often cited as the principal reason for our current trade deficit. But if we had merely retained our former share of world exports, our trade balance would have remained strongly positive, even in the face of rising oil costs.

Among seventeen major manufacturing categories, we have lost export market share in all seventeen, while Germany and Japan have gained share in fourteen. Among 102 manufactured products analyzed in a recent government report, the United States has lost export share in 71. Even in agriculture, our most successful export industry, our share of world soybean exports has declined from 96 percent to less than 70 percent.

• Perhaps most disturbing, by the late 1970s, our balance of trade with the NICs in manufactured goods had fallen to a disappointing negative $3 billion. Our inability to penetrate these fast-growing markets is an especially black augury for our future.

• In the past, the United States maintained its economic and industrial position through modest but consistently superior productivity growth.* For eighty years between 1870 and 1950, American productivity (gross national product per worker) grew only seven-tenths of one percent faster than that of Europe and Japan. This small, indeed almost negligible margin, propelled us from obscurity to the first rank of world powers. Yet for the postwar period as a whole, Japan's and West Germany's productivity has outstripped ours by margins of 3 to 6 percent per year.

The results of this fundamental change have been dramatic. Ford Motor Company has released a comparison of relatively efficient Ford plants with competing Toyota plants. The Ford plants produce two engines per day per employee versus nine for Toyota. A similar study of the color television industry revealed that American labor costs per set were twice as high as in Japan even though Japanese workers were better paid.

• The key to maintaining national productivity lies in constant and wise investment of national savings. In both

---

*Much of the macroeconomic data used in this chapter was generously provided by Peter G. Peterson, chairman of the board, Lehman Brothers Kuhn Loeb, and former secretary of commerce under President Nixon.

savings and investment, however, the American record has been dismal. The average American family used to save about 5 percent of income. Today it is closer to zero. By contrast, the average Japanese family saves 20 percent of its income and the average West German family saves 15 percent.

American industry draws upon its own and the public's savings to invest about 10 percent of gross national product per year in new plant and equipment. This is the worst performance of any major industrial country including Great Britain. In 1981, Japan invested more than all of American industry combined, even though Japan's gross national product is only half as large as ours.

Inevitably, our plant and equipment are older than our competitors'. Whatever initial advantage Germany and Japan gained by rebuilding from the rubble of World War Two, they compounded their advantage by continuing to rebuild. As of 1978, German and Japanese manufacturing plants were only ten to twelve years old on average versus sixteen to seventeen years old in the United States. In specific export industries such as steel, the comparison is even more stark. Over 70 percent of Japanese steel is produced by modern continuous casting methods versus only 16 percent of American steel.

• Just as important as quantity of investment is quality of investment. One aspect of quality is the ability to innovate. In the past, the United States devoted a greater share of its gross national product to industrial research and development than any other Western nation. Today we trail West Germany and Japan.

Nor is there much hope for improvement in the near future. As Japanese businessmen repeatedly stressed to Peter Drucker, noted American business philosopher and professor, on a recent trip to Japan: "You in the United States have in the last ten years doubled the number of people in law schools, while you barely even maintained the number of people in engineering schools. We in Japan have not increased the number of lawyers but have doubled the number of engineering students. Lawyers are concerned with dividing the pie, engineers with making it larger."

Faced with these facts, even the most friendly and optimistic observer of America could hardly avoid a diagnosis of severe if not yet terminal decline. At the same time, concepts such as GNP growth, world market share, industry market share, and export market share are abstractions. So are productivity, national savings and investment, and innovation. One might well ask what failure in these areas actually means for the United States and for individual Americans.

At one level, it means declining personal income. As recently as 1968, our gross national product per person was the highest in the world. By 1979, we had fallen to eighth place. Adjusted for inflation, the average American worker earned less in the late seventies than in the late sixties. If present trends continue, our leading competitors such as Japan and West Germany could enjoy twice our standard of living by the end of the century.

At a deeper level, our economic and industrial failure involves a fundamental change in the world balance of power. So long as the United States maintained its industrial superiority, we could be sure that our nation and our values would survive and prosper. As our power wanes, friendly nations such as Germany and Japan may pick up the reins of world leadership and carry on in our stead, but there are reasons to doubt whether any other Western nation will be able to assume the leadership role we have filled. In the absence of such leadership, the world will almost certainly be a less stable—and perhaps less safe—place in which to live.

2 The Alibis

Why is the American collapse taking place? Who is responsible? Two answers are commonly offered. The first is to blame America's industrial decline on the Organization of Petroleum Exporting Countries (OPEC). The second is to accuse the Japanese and others of exploiting the United States by failing to shoulder a fair share of our common defense burden and by excluding our goods from their markets. In each case, there is at least some measure of truth. But neither of these answers, either singly or together, adequately explains our failing competitiveness.

Obviously the OPEC oil cartel has had a major impact on our economy. In 1965 a barrel of foreign oil cost less than $2. Today the price is over $30. These prices have increased the cost of American oil imports from $4.3 billion in 1972 to $74 billion in 1980. As Felix Rohatyn, a partner of one of New York's leading investment banks, has pointed out, the market value of all companies listed on the New York Stock Exchange is $1.2 trillion. This enormous wealth, built up over two centuries, now represents just sixteen years of payments to OPEC. Given this fact alone, it is easy to blame our economic problems on the Arabs and other cartel members.

To do so, however, is to fail to understand the scope of the problem. Japan and West Germany have both managed to strengthen their trade balances despite overwhelming dependence on OPEC. Both countries must import more than 90 percent of their oil. The United States by contrast has substantial petroleum reserves (we are the third-largest producer of oil in the world) and currently imports about 50 percent of its oil. If we were as frugal and efficient in our use of energy as Europe and Japan, we would not have to import any oil at all. Despite this advantage, we have had a harder time adjusting to OPEC price increases than our leading competitors.

The case of Japan is instructive. Between 1973 and 1978, Japan's oil trade deficit increased by $31 billion. In addition, the country's shortfall in other natural resources and in food rose by $20 billion. In all, Japan had to absorb negative trade balances in basic commodities of over $50 billion. Any other country would have been staggered by this burden. Instead, Japan increased its exports of manufactured goods from $13 billion in 1970 to $77 billion in 1978. The result was 3.2 million additional jobs for Japanese workers and an even stronger trade position.

While energy is very important, it is not the root cause of our troubles. Unless we return to nineteenth century imperialism, high OPEC prices are simply a fact of life. They make us poorer and the Arabs richer. The answer for the United States is to keep our dollars at home by raising prices high enough to generate conservation, more production, more use of coal, and faster development of alternative energy sources. In this respect, the most radical members of OPEC, the greediest price hawks, ironically have been our very best friends. Energy prices would have risen without them, albeit more gradually. By shocking us, not once but repeatedly, they forced us finally to decontrol our prices and begin the long process of regaining our energy independence.

After the Arabs, the second most common whipping boys for American failure have been our allies, especially the Japanese. A major area of contention has been defense spending. In 1981, the United States devoted 5.2 percent of its gross national product to defense versus 3.3 percent for Germany, 3.9 percent for France, and 0.9

percent for Japan. Japanese businessmen reportedly spent more on entertainment than their government budgeted for defense. Despite these figures, European and Japanese defense expenditures grew more rapidly in the seventies than did ours. In addition, American allies purchased up to $4.5 billion worth of military aircraft and other equipment per year from the United States. If allied defense spending rose to U.S. levels but shifted to domestic supply sources, our overall trade balance would suffer.

Another area of concern has been trade barriers. American farmers complain that prohibitive tariffs shut out their products from Japanese markets. As a result, sirloin sells for $45 a pound in Tokyo and Florida oranges for $1 each. American businessmen also cite nontariff barriers such as onerous reporting and testing requirements, irrational safety rules, and even cultural prejudices. In one egregious example, the Japanese Tobacco, Alcohol, and Salt Monopoly, a government corporation, has issued byzantine regulations which restrict American cigarettes to only 14,000 of 250,000 potential outlets. Similarly, American automobile manufacturers are forced to make trivial changes in their catalytic converters even though these changes add an additional $250 to eventual sales price. The rationale offered by the Japanese government for this requirement is that refitted converters reduce heat and thus guard against fires along country lanes.

The story, however, has another side. The Congressional Budget Office has reported that the average tariff rate for imports into Japan is now lower than for imports into the United States. While the Japanese have sharply reduced their trade barriers in recent years, the United States has established or increased trade barriers against such goods as textiles, sugar, beef, shoes, citizen band radios, steel, and autos. The International Monetary Fund has identified ninety-two separate actions taken by the American government in recent years to restrict imports.

Perhaps the most telling evidence against the Japanese Trade Conspiracy Theory is our steadily declining share of Japanese imports. As the Japanese government has lifted trade barriers and allowed increased imports, American sales should have grown along with the market. Instead, U.S. firms lost market share across a wide range of industries including agriculture, capital equipment, chemicals, and textiles. Total market share losses in Japan have added $3 billion to our current trade deficit.

The most substantial and inexplicable loss in our trade with Japan has been coal. As a heavily industrialized country with few natural resources, Japan imports large amounts of coal for energy. The United States, with its massive coal reserves, has always been a major supplier. Yet during the 1970s, the American share of Japanese imports fell from about one half to one third. This alone increased our trade imbalance by an additional $1 billion.

As the Boston Consulting Group pointed out in an independent study for the Treasury Department: "The fact that the United States is losing its share of the Japanese market in most categories of Japanese imports puts the trade balance issue into a rather different perspective. Trade barriers cannot explain these data. Whatever the barriers, the United States is supplying a smaller part of what Japan does in fact take in. This is the case despite the United States' advantages over other suppliers—a long history of close trade association; much the highest level of foreign investment in Japan; and close strategic association."

American business can do better. As late as 1981, total American investment in Japan was still only one-tenth as large as American investment in Great Britain, a smaller, more mature, and less dynamic market. Very few

American companies have made the large-scale and long-term commitment necessary for success in the Far East. Yet even so, Japan accounted for less than a third of our overall trade deficit in 1980. Our problem simply cannot be explained by relations with any single competitor.

The evidence is thus clear. Neither the Arabs nor the Japanese are to blame for our declining competitiveness. To find the real reasons for our current industrial malaise, we must look both backward and within—to the United States of the mid-1960s.

3 The New Industrial State Revisited

> . . . The ideas of economists and political phi-
> losophers, both when they are right and when
> they are wrong, are more powerful than is com-
> monly understood. Indeed the world is ruled by
> little else. Practical men, who believe themselves
> to be quite exempt from any intellectual
> influences, are usually the slaves of some
> defunct economist.
>
> —JOHN MAYNARD KEYNES

In 1967, John Kenneth Galbraith published a book on the American economy called *The New Industrial State.* A former president of the American Economic Association, Galbraith had only recently returned to Harvard after serving as President Kennedy's ambassador to India. His book was widely hailed and immediately became an international bestseller. Even now, over fifteen years later, it is the place to begin in understanding our continuing industrial decline.

Galbraith's message can be readily summarized. American corporations, he argued, had grown ever larger in order to accommodate the vast quantities of capital and technology required for industrial success. Several hundred "technically dynamic, massively capitalized, highly organized" companies represented the "heartland" of the American economy. Examples included General Motors, Ford, Chrysler, Texaco, Gulf, U.S. Steel, DuPont, and Western Electric. Other companies, especially small companies, mattered little or not at all.

In Galbraith's "heartland," traditional entrepreneurship had disappeared. Indeed, it was no longer needed.
Capitalists had been replaced by technocrats. Business
managers viewed themselves primarily as scientists and
engineers. Corporate directors were as likely to be university presidents as bankers. Such technocratic leaders
no longer sought to maximize profits either over the short
or long term. Their primary goal was to create security
and certainty by insulating themselves from change. To a
remarkable degree, they had succeeded in doing so.

Large companies no longer depended on either shareholders or banks for funding. Retained earnings, that
part of profits not paid out in corporate dividends, provided all the money that was needed. Such companies
had also largely eliminated the threat of competition.
Important industries had been carved up by a few like-
minded concerns. Since both radical product innovations
and price cutting were frowned on, the only permissible
form of competition lay in advertising. If a smaller company in an industry dared to buck the system, it would be
swiftly and savagely punished by the larger companies.
None of this, of course, was ever discussed. To do so
would have broken antitrust laws. It was simply understood.

Freed from the perils of overt competition, companies
could also abandon the traditional struggle against labor
union wage demands. On the whole, the easier course
was simply to give in to labor and pass the costs on to the
customer. If customer demand flagged because of high
prices, sales could always be restored by offering new
brands and slight product modifications and by manipu-
lating the public through mass advertising campaigns.

In effect, the market as defined by economists had
been quietly shelved. In its place was a tightly disciplined
world in which industry dictated that the public buy
redundant and often useless products at controlled
prices. Even government, long an adversary of business,

had been co-opted by the system. Its role was to reduce uncertainty even further by maintaining a stable economy and enforcing antitrust laws as little as possible. In return, industry rewarded public officials (scientists, engineers, and educators like themselves) with political support and high-paying jobs. Capitalism in its new form was still distinguishable from socialism or communism. But modern societies of all kinds had grown increasingly alike and would probably converge further as time passed.

Galbraith's book was intended to be about the future. Like many books about the future, however, it turned out to be about the past. *The New Industrial State* described, in exaggerated form, the mature American economy of the mid-sixties. Already by 1967 this world was in rapid decline. By the seventies, it would be utterly devastated by trends that Galbraith failed to note.

One of these trends was the emergence of new companies and new technologies in such fields as semiconductors, computers, and telecommunications.* Another was the accelerating transfer of American capital (through foreign aid and commercial loans) and American technology (through foreign plants and licenses) to other countries around the world. The combination of capital, technology, and lower wage rates produced formidable competition, especially in basic industries. A third trend was the toppling of long-standing trade barriers through a series of critically important trade negotiations. The Kennedy Round of 1962–67 reduced tariffs on industrial goods among developed nations by a third on average. The Tokyo Round of 1976 produced another 40 percent reduction. Finally, the oil price shocks of 1973 and 1979 convinced even the United States of its dependence on foreign trade. The result of all these trends was

---

*Of the "heartland" companies which Galbraith specifically cited, none became leaders in these fields. The index to the New Industrial state lists eleven references to General Motors, none to IBM.

the emergence of a new global marketplace that dwarfed the parochial American economy described in Galbraith's book. In only fifteen years, between 1965 and 1980, a new world came into being.

The United States contributed as much as any other nation to the development of this world, and Americans could have benefited from the resulting changes. Unfortunately, our attitudes and policies remained stuck in the Galbraithian mold. In his other writings, Galbraith suggested that government de-emphasize economic growth as a national goal. He also recommended price controls and vigorous action to rein in the power of large corporations. Throughout the seventies, both Republican and Democratic administrations either adopted or experimented with each of these ideas. Companies that might have cut prices to meet foreign competition remembered the Nixon price freeze and were deterred.* Strong international competitors such as IBM, Xerox, AT&T, and even U.S. Steel were harassed by actual or potential antitrust suits because of their domestic market size.

If government alone had been at fault, the damage might have been contained. In fact, however, private industry was equally backward-looking. By the late sixties, many major American companies had become more comfortable with Galbraithian assumptions than they cared to admit. They had fought hard through the decades to win a dominant share of an important market. They had constantly reinvested to maintain their position through years of dramatic growth. Finally growth had slowed, investment requirements subsided, and cash began to flow. This should have been a stable and untroubled harvest time. Instead, the market suddenly and unexpectedly redefined itself. A dominant share of

---

*Faced with the possibility of government price controls, corporate managers will usually raise prices as much as possible to provide a margin of safety against future cost increases.

an American industry became only a toehold in an international industry. Growth and tremendous investment demands started all over again.

Many companies simply failed to respond. They either could not or would not grasp what was taking place around them. They failed to invest. If they did invest, they spread limited resources through too many businesses. They failed to plow profits back into automation and cost control. They refused to cut prices to deter foreign competitors. As Robert Hayes and William Abernathy, both Harvard Business School professors, have noted: "American management in the two decades after World War Two was . . . admired for . . . its performance. But times change. An approach shaped and refined during stable decades may be ill suited to a world characterized by rapid and unpredictable change, scarce energy, global competition for markets, and a constant need for innovation. This is the world of the 1980s and, probably, the rest of the century."

Even the initial attempts of American managers to internationalize were often misguided. When they moved into Europe, they set up separate subsidiary companies and plants in each major country. As a result, individual plants were often too small to make full use of advanced technology. By the time tariffs fell to the low levels of the Tokyo Round, many companies had missed the chance to consolidate their production in a few places and take full advantage of critical scale economies.

Who then is responsible for America's lack of competitiveness? The answer is unavoidable. Americans—both in government and industry—have created their own problems by living in the past and by pursuing outdated and misguided policies. The days when the United States represented the greatest free-trade zone and market in the world are now over. The time has come to move ahead and make our lives in the international markets of the future.

4 The OECD Report

Time present and time past
Are both perhaps present in the time future
And time future contained in time past
— T. S. Eliot, "Burnt Norton"

One of the most elite clubs in the world is the Organization for Economic Cooperation and Development (OECD). It includes among its members the very richest industrial nations. During the late 1970s, the Council of OECD authorized "Facing the Future," a multiyear study of the "development of advanced industrial societies in harmony with that of developing countries." The project involved staff from nineteen different OECD members and was funded by major international foundations.

Here are a few highlights:

1. Human population will triple from four to twelve billion within a century. It will then become essentially stationary. By the end of this century, Europe will have hardly grown at all. Brazil and Indonesia will have almost as many people as the United States. Virtually all population growth in the Soviet Union will be outside Russia proper in the nonwhite Asiatic republics. In all, over 80 percent of the world's population will be concentrated in developing nations. As a direct result, labor will continue to be very cheap, a potential source of comparative advantage for countries able to exploit it.

THE TWENTY MOST POPULOUS COUNTRIES
IN THE YEAR 2000
(IN MILLIONS)

Rank	*2000*	*1970*
1. China	1148	722
2. India	1059	543
3. USSR	315	243
4. USA	264	205
5. Indonesia	238	119
6. Brazil	213	95
7. Pakistan	147	60
8. Bangladesh	144	68
9. Nigeria	135	55
10. Japan	133	104
11. Mexico	132	50
12. Philippines	90	38
13. Thailand	86	36
14. Vietnam	76	39
15. Turkey	73	35
16. Iran	67	NA
17. Germany	66	61
18. Egypt	65	NA
19. United Kingdom	63	55
20. France	62	51

2. Economic growth will continue throughout the world for the next half century without encountering insurmountable limits. *Both energy and natural resources will be in sufficient supply.* Growth, however, will be at a slower rate than during the last thirty years.

3. A new generation of industries will gradually take the place of those responsible for the postwar expansion. "Four great technological adventures are under way: in electronics (teleprocessing and automation); in biology, with a whole array of effects on health and on agricul-

tural and industrial activities; in energy production, with the development of alternative major sources of primary energy; and finally in the use of the oceans and space." Competition among developed countries for control of these new industries will be intense. Governments as well as companies will participate. Some governments on the losing end of this struggle will feel internal pressure to withdraw from world markets. However, the internationalization of trade will make this increasingly difficult.

4. Major geographic power shifts will take place. The United States' share of world income will continue to decline. Europe will also lose share. Asia could become the center of the world economy. Within Asia, Japan will remain the dominant factor. The fast-growing Asian developing countries—Taiwan, South Korea, Hong Kong, Singapore, and Malaysia—will represent another power bloc. The Philippines and perhaps Indonesia might also eventually join this new "coprosperity sphere." China, under new leadership, could also become a critical force in the world economy.

With these basic findings in mind, the OECD staff prepared a series of alternative scenarios covering the next twenty years of economic development. Scenario A assumed a reasonably high world growth rate of 5 percent a year with an ever more rapid expansion of international trade. Scenario B was similar except that growth proceeded at a slower pace. Scenario C was premised on a conflict-ridden world in which economic relations break down between the industrialized world and the developing world. This would represent an especially negative environment for Japan because of that country's need for Third World resources and markets. Finally, Scenario D assumed a return to protectionism and the emergence of three regional trading zones centered in Europe, the United States, and Japan. Growth in both world gross national product and international trade would be reduced. What is notable about all four scenarios is that *the United States loses ground in each.* No matter what environment unfolds, the authors of the report expect the American decline to continue.

SHARE OF WORLD GROSS NATIONAL PRODUCT

Competitor	Year 1975	Year 2000A	Year 2000B	Year 2000C	Year 2000D
United States	29	19	18	24	21
Japan	7	10	10	5	9
Europe (Common Market)	18	16	14	13	14
Other Western Nations	8	8	8	6	7
Eastern Europe	16	16	18	19	17
Third World	22	31	32	33	32
TOTAL	100	100	100	100	100

Looking solely at OECD members, the report predicts that the United States (under Scenario A) will have the worst productivity growth of any industrial nation.

AVERAGE ANNUAL PRODUCTIVITY GROWTH TO THE YEAR 2000

Country	%	Country	%
Japan	6.2	United Kingdom	3.3
Italy	5.5	Sweden	3.2
Germany	4.1	Australia	3.1
France	4.1	New Zealand	3.0
Netherlands	4.1	Canada	2.3
Belgium	3.9	United States	2.2*

The OECD report provides an objective outside evaluation of America's future. It was not written by Eastern

*Actually 1.8 percent after adjustment for low base year of 1975. Since American productivity growth in 1975 was unusually low, it distorted the twenty-five-year projection upward.

bloc or even Third World economists with a political ax to grind. It was written by America's friends. The report's conclusion is therefore all the more telling: "The United States has ceased to be exceptional."

5 The Next Round

The OECD report is not the only study predicting darker days ahead for American industry. Alan Greenspan, former chairman of the Council of Economic Advisors under President Ford, has projected a major American merchandise trade deficit for every single year of the 1980s. Various experts have cited the following obstacles to eventual American recovery:

THE SHADOW OF OPEC

The second oil price shock of 1979 left many nations virtually destitute. In all, developing nations without major oil reserves have borrowed over $450 billion to pay for oil or capital projects. Egypt has mortgaged over 69 percent of its entire gross national product; Zambia 67 percent; South Korea 29 percent, and Kenya 26 percent. Such countries must export to survive. Although they will continue to buy from the United States, their means will be limited.

UNSUSTAINABLE AGRICULTURAL EXPORTS

During the 1970s, American agricultural exports grew 9 percent per year faster than total exports and helped to offset our mounting trade deficit. By 1980, our agricultural trade surplus reached a record $23 billion, over twenty times our surplus in 1969.

Unfortunately, this rate of growth was sustained by unusual circumstances, including crop failures in Russia, China, Africa, the Middle East, and India as well as record harvests at home. For the next ten years, the most likely scenario is for our agricultural exports to continue at high levels, but to grow even more slowly than our other exports.

A SHRUNKEN MANUFACTURING EXPORT BASE

Following World War Two, the United States enjoyed a strong trade balance in a wide variety of major industries. Today, however, the number of major industries with trade surpluses is limited. Of the fifty American companies with the largest export volume, seventeen sell high-technology capital goods such as airplanes, computers, and other electronic equipment. Another nine sell less advanced capital equipment such as agricultural and construction machinery. Another thirteen are involved with chemicals. In dollar terms, five aerospace firms alone represent 20 percent of the total.

Such concentration is not necessarily disadvantageous. It could be justified if American companies were fully exploiting their areas of strength. The reality, however, is quite different. Of the fifty exporters, two are in serious financial condition. Virtually all are losing world market share. Under these circumstances, the loss of a single key industry such as aerospace or chemicals would be disastrous for our future trade position.

NEW AND STRONG COMPETITORS

Although America's export base has shrunk, the number of our competitors has multiplied. In agriculture, there is an increasingly productive South America. In the chemical industry, there will soon be major Arab competitors. With so many chemicals manufactured from a petroleum base, the logic of Arab competition is inexorable. In basic and consumer industries, there are Hong Kong, Singapore, Taiwan, South Korea, Brazil, and Mexico. These newly industrialized countries (NICs) have gained access to standardized Western technology. By saving and investing a large share of their national incomes, they are adding new plant and equipment at a rapid rate. The combination of high savings and low wages will not last forever. As in the case of Japan, wage rates will eventually rise with economic growth. But directly behind the NICs are another group of aspirants including Malaysia, the Philippines, Indonesia, Kenya, and perhaps even China. Other groups will doubtless form in the future.

For as far ahead as anyone can see, Western industries will be threatened by a veritable tide of cheap labor. Mexico, with all its new oil wealth, still suffers an unemployment rate in excess of 30 percent. China must find work for an additional seventy to a hundred million people in the next few decades. Wages in Mexico, Hong Kong, and Singapore are currently only one-fourth to one-twelfth what they are here. Even by the end of the century, Chinese wages may be only one-twentieth of ours. If Chinese productivity improves and reaches a level one-fifth or even one-fourth as great as ours, unit labor costs would still be four or five times lower than in the United States.

ASSAULT IN HIGH TECHNOLOGY

Japanese and European leaders often argue that their nations are even more vulnerable than the United States to emerging Third World competition. With Japanese and European exports concentrated in older industries and with rising Japanese and German wages (German laborers now earn 20 percent more on average than their American counterparts), they may be right.

Japanese and European counterstrategies are not, however, designed to ease American anxieties. In each case, government-sanctioned plans are to move the country's industrial base "upscale" by assaulting American dominance in high-technology fields such as semiconductors and computers.

A leading edge in these fields is expected to produce more export earnings through the sale of computers, telecommunication equipment, and other advanced electronic equipment and components. Just as importantly, computer technology can be used to automate basic and consumer manufacturing plants and thus stem Third World advances. The Japanese do not yet know whether an automobile plant run by industrial robots and computers will ultimately be able to compete with Third World labor, but in a worst-case scenario, precious time can be gained. And in the best case, fully automated plants may be able to produce competitively priced cars for the balance of this century.

Japanese and European plans are reasonable, well-developed, and bold. Unfortunately, they can only succeed at our expense. The most crucial battle for world markets in the next several decades will thus continue to be with Japan and Europe. By the end of the century, either Japan, Europe, or the United States will be supreme in high technology. Depending on the decisiveness of the outcome, the losers could face a vastly diminished future.

Faced with reduced export markets, a shrunken industrial export base, new Third World competitors, and Japanese/European plans to storm our last industrial strongholds, the United States cannot afford to remain confused, passive, or vulnerable. We must abandon once and for all the idea that our current difficulties are temporary and will resolve themselves in time. Although this should be obvious after a decade of decline, significant numbers of American businessmen remain unconcerned. Only 10 percent of American manufacturing companies bother to export. Just one hundred companies represent half of all our overseas trade.

Even government officials are divided in their views of the situation. While many government officials appreciate the importance of international markets, many do not. In a paper prepared for the president's "Report on U.S. Competitiveness in 1980," Dale W. Larson of the Department of the Treasury wrote that "Policies designed to increase investment, research and development, and productivity, or to curb inflation should be pursued if they will increase domestic income and welfare, but not to meet foreign competition. If the domestic economy is performing well, the trade accounts will take care of themselves." Trade accounts are influenced by currency fluctuations and other short-term factors and are thus an incomplete measure of American competitiveness. Even allowing for this fact, however, the reversal of Larson's statement would more nearly be true. If American export competitiveness is assured, the domestic economy will take care of itself.

Simply recognizing the severity and magnitude of America's current problems is a critical first step toward their solution. At the same time, the United States needs a strategic consensus about what to do next. One option is a return to protectionism. Except for the European Common Market, the United States is still the largest free trade zone in the world. With our strong natural resource base, we are less dependent on imports than many other developed nations. If we felt convinced that we could not compete in the global economy and that our decline was irrevocable, our leaders would be wrong to exclude protectionism as an alternative.

The cost of a protectionist strategy would, however, be substantial. By shutting our borders, we could easily set off an international depression. Even without a depression, we would experience massive industrial dislocation, unemployment, and slower economic activity. Since the dismantling of an international marketplace would reduce everyone's growth prospects, including our own, protectionism is obviously a desperate remedy. Another option, the reverse of protectionism, is that the United States become a specialist in technological innovation and let the rest of the world supply our remaining wants. The theory behind this approach has been summarized in a Labor Department report:

> . . . Countries with substantial research and development resources and a large and sophisticated internal market will first develop and produce high technology goods for the home market and for export. Initially such goods will be very capital intensive, but as product development progresses and the production technology becomes standardized, production will tend to move abroad to countries which can acquire the technology and which have lower labor costs. . . . Unless the developers of technology can prevent its diffusion, they can expect to lose their competitive advantage to other countries. A corollary is that to maintain a comparative strength in high technology products, a country must constantly invest in sophisticated basic research.

According to this theory of technological transfer, the United States has already irrevocably lost its basic and consumer industries. It is only a matter of time before we lose computers, aerospace, telecommunications, and other advanced industries as well. Only agriculture will remain because of our unique natural resources. To prevent long-term decline, we must therefore constantly renew ourselves by creating new technologies and products.

Technological specialization is a seductive but highly

doubtful strategy. The underlying theory—a staple of economics textbooks—may turn out to be entirely wrong. Production technologies, once standardized, do not necessarily remain forever frozen. The Japanese are betting billions of dollars that they can revolutionize the production of automobiles with robots and so-called computer-aided design and manufacturing (CAD/CAM), and thus offset the lower labor costs of their NIC competitors. Although the Japanese lead in robots, the United States leads in CAD/CAM. If the Japanese can save their basic industries through automation, we should be able to salvage some of ours.

Other objections to technological specialization are even more fundamental. For military reasons alone, the United States cannot afford to give up its capability in steel or autos. A national portfolio comprised solely of new growth-industries would also require billions, even trillions, of investment dollars. Where would the funds be found if not in successful, stable, and cash-rich older industries? Finally, the assumption of constant and ever accelerating technological change contradicts human nature. Because we live in an era of technological hyperactivity, we assume that the current pace is sustainable. In fact, as economic historians have noted, technological change tends to come in waves. At some point the rate of innovation pauses for a period of years or decades before resuming at a later date.

If neither protectionism nor technological specialization makes sense, that leaves only one broad option. It is to battle foreign competition simultaneously on a variety of fronts. This does not mean that the United States should try to lead in every industry. Specialization within each agricultural, basic, consumer, high-technology, and emerging technology sector is essential. But our goal should be to dominate at least a few industries in each sector.

Moreover, we must clearly redefine dominance to mean international dominance. Our way of thinking and even of keeping economic statistics must be completely overhauled. At present, no one knows exactly how much of the world mainframe computer market is controlled by American companies. The government makes no effort to generate or publish such data. We do know the market share of American companies within the United States, the total American share of world exports, and industry trade balances. What counts, however, is total international production, and neither the Commerce Department nor the president's trade representative seem to be interested in this figure. It is symptomatic of a much broader gap in public and official understanding.

Once the United States has committed itself to a broad-scale battle for world market share, a number of specific changes in business and public policy would be helpful. For example, American business should abandon its traditional approach to profits and profitability, and the federal government should review and preferably eliminate most antitrust statutes. These and other changes enumerated in later chapters are long overdue. Together with a broader strategic understanding, they could yet reverse the decline in American fortunes.

Even the most respected economic forecasts—whether from the OECD or a former chairman of the President's Council of Economic Advisors—can be proven wrong. The combination of a new world-market together with a variety of new technologies creates opportunity as well as unpredictability. To borrow a phrase from Joseph Schumpeter, one of the greatest economists of this century, we have entered a period of "creative destruction." These periods "incessantly revolutionize the economic structure from within, incessantly destroying the old one, incessantly creating a new one." When the gales of destruction abate, a new era will have dawned. Whether the United States will still lead the world during that era depends on our willingness to fight and win the specific battles described in the balance of this book.

Part Two

The Technology Front

6 "Crude Oil" of the 1980s

America's future as an industrial power is dependent on a tiny silicon chip known as a semiconductor. No larger than a postage stamp, such chips are capable of storing enormous amounts of information. They are the key to the electronic age and the foundation upon which dozens of industries are being built.

A semiconductor is a small piece of solid material, usually silicon, that conducts electricity in a single direction and that can be used to store electronic data. Up to 65,000 bits of information can be stored on a single chip. This information can then be recalled on command and used for a variety of purposes. There are many different types of semiconductors, some more sophisticated than others. They range from simple transistors used in televisions and radios to scientifically advanced chips that are really miniature computers.

Semiconductor technology first emerged in 1947 when William Shockley, John Bardeen, and Walter Brattain of Bell Laboratories invented the transistor. The transistor performed all the electronic amplifying and switching functions previously performed by the vacuum tube, but was more powerful, more durable, used less energy, and was substantially smaller. The development of the transistor constituted a major technological breakthrough. For their work the three Bell scientists received the Nobel Prize in Physics.

Semiconductor technology took another step forward in 1959 when Texas Instruments and Fairchild Camera both announced that they had successfully manufactured integrated circuits. Integrated circuits were created by reducing the size of transistors so that several could be placed on the same piece of silicon. Large-scale integration, which came later in the 1960s, was another major development in chip technology. This involved placing over one hundred interconnected transistors on a single chip, thereby allowing a semiconductor to perform more than one function.

The 1970s began with an announcement by Intel Corporation, located in California's famed "Silicon Valley" near San Francisco, that it had developed two powerful new types of semiconductors called the random access memory (RAM) and the microprocessor. The first random access memory was called the 1K RAM. It could store more than one thousand pieces of information on a single chip. The microprocessor was essentially a "computer on a chip." It combined arithmetic and logic functions and could be programmed to perform a wide variety of tasks.

Today's semiconductors are even further advanced. RAMs are being sold that store over 64,000 pieces of information. Microprocessor advances have also been profound. In 1981 both Intel and Hewlett-Packard announced that they had developed a new microprocessor with the computational power of a large computer. Intel claims that its microprocessor, priced at $10,000, has equivalent computing power to an IBM 370 machine costing $2 million.

The tremendous advances made in semiconductor technology since the development of the transistor have completely revolutionized the computer industry. The world's first electronic computer (the Electronic Numerical Integrator and Calculator of 1946) required nearly 20,000 vacuum tubes to operate and weighed thirty tons. Today a single microprocessor, weighing less than one ounce, is twenty times more powerful.

As semiconductor technology has advanced, so have its possible applications. Although computer companies use over 40 percent of all chips produced, semiconductors are also used in air conditioners, refrigerators, cameras, pocket calculators, digital watches, typewriters, telephones, electronic toys, stereos, home appliances, airplanes, automobiles, and machine tools. According to the Department of Commerce, chip technology is now used in the production of more than $200 billion worth of goods and services in the United States alone. As more uses have been found for semiconductors, international demand for chips has skyrocketed. The production of semiconductors doubled every year during the 1970s. Total world sales increased from $1 billion to $13 billion.

As semiconductors have become mass produced products, their price has fallen rapidly. The price per function of an integrated circuit fell by almost 30 percent a year during the 1970s. The average price of a transistor, which sold for about $10 in 1960, is now less than one cent.

Use of semiconductors should increase even further in the 1980s and 1990s. The Department of Commerce expects that the world market for semiconductors will exceed $50 billion by 1988 and $200 billion by the end of the century.

The automobile industry is just one area where semiconductor technology will become increasingly important. Hard pressed to meet federally mandated fuel economies by 1985, Detroit is relying heavily on the use of microprocessors to improve engine efficiency. Every new car produced by General Motors in 1981 had at least two microprocessors under its hood. Microprocessors have been designed that measure and automatically adjust engine speed, temperature, and pressure. General Motors predicts that 30 to 40 million American cars will have such systems by 1985. It is estimated that automobile industry demand for microprocessors will double to more than $1 billion by 1985.

The demand for semiconductors is also expected to grow significantly in industries where chips are already in wide use. In computers, semiconductors currently account for about 6 percent of the product's cost but this percentage should double by 1990. In other electronic equipment as well, semiconductors will represent a larger part of the final product.

The semiconductor market has unlimited potential. As Jerry Sanders, president of Advanced Micro Devices Inc., has pointed out, semiconductors are important enough to be regarded as the "crude oil" of the 1980s. It is crucial for American industry to be at the forefront of this technology.

7 Assault on Silicon Valley

American companies have dominated the semiconductor industry from its inception. In recent years, however, Japanese manufacturers have begun to challenge our world leadership. Charles E. Sporck, president of National Semiconductor Corporation, has warned that "Japanese companies intend to dominate the U.S. semiconductor industry just as similar efforts have overtaken many other American industries."

During the 1960s, the Japanese government targeted semiconductors as a critical growth industry of the future. The powerful Ministry of International Trade and Industry (MITI) provided grants of over $250 million to help get the industry on its feet. The government also relaxed antitrust laws so that firms could pool their knowledge and resources in research and product development. Additionally, MITI's own Electronics Research Institute directly pursued the advancement of semiconductor technology.

With such government assistance, Japanese firms have captured more than 20 percent of the world market for chips. Our own share has declined from a high of almost 90 percent in the early 1960s to 60 precent in 1980. In the market for 16K RAMS, which provide the core memory for most computers made today, Japan is now the world leader with 40 percent of the American market alone.

American manufacturers can blame only themselves for letting the Japanese establish themselves in the 16K

RAM market. The largest U.S. computer and semiconductor firms significantly underestimated the demand for RAMs in the late 1970s and were not able to add capacity quickly enough to meet the tremendous backlog of orders that developed. Demand was so great that some semiconductor manufacturers had waiting lists of up to one year. Rather than wait this long, buyers turned to Japanese firms. Even the leading American semiconductor manufacturers had to buy from the Japanese. In the late 1970s, IBM, Intel, and Texas Instruments were each buying more than one million RAMs a year from Japan.

Given the opportunity to enter the U.S. market, the Japanese made the most of it. Japanese semiconductor sales in the United States leaped from $62 million in 1977 to $370 million in 1980. Two large Japanese chipmakers, Hitachi and Fujitsu, built their own semiconductor plants here. Two other major Japanese competitors, Nippon Electric and Toshiba, purchased American semiconductor companies as a way of acquiring additional technological expertise and increasing semiconductor production capacity. Nippon Electric also laid plans to build a $100 million semiconductor plant in Roseville, California.

The Japanese competitive strategy centered on quality. By spending more time and money on quality control than their American rivals, they managed to manufacture exceptionally reliable chips. This produced a significant competitive advantage because replacing defective components can be both a major headache and expense for computer manufacturers. In tests conducted by Hewlett-Packard, the failure rate of the best-made Japanese chips was only one-sixth as great as for comparable American products. For lower-quality chips, the Japanese failure rate was only one twenty-seventh as great.

Japanese firms are also beginning to make breakthroughs in semiconductor technology. In recent years,

Japanese semiconductor manufacturers have spent 12 to 13 percent of their total sales revenues on R&D in addition to government funded programs. This compares to the 6 or 7 percent of sales which U.S. firms have spent on R&D.

Japanese research expenditures began paying off in 1978 when Fujitsu became the first firm in the world to market the 64K RAM, the memory for the next generation of computers. Since then, four other Japanese companies have begun producing 64K RAMs. Today Hitachi controls nearly 40 percent of the world market for these chips. American companies with competitive chips include Texas Instruments, National Semiconductor, Intel, and Mostek. Although the battle is still in its early stages, the Japanese have captured 70 percent of the market.

If the Japanese maintain their lead in the 64K RAM market, it could have devastating implications for the future of our semiconductor industry. RAMs are high-volume, mass-produced products that provide the necessary cash flow to support research and development expenditures. Fred Bucy, president of Texas Instruments, has already warned that the spiraling cost of production equipment and research and development will make it increasingly difficult for American firms to maintain their world leadership in semiconductors in future years. He forecasts that American companies will have to spend between $25 and $35 billion during the 1980s—compared to $4 billion invested in the 1970s—to preserve their current market position.

American semiconductor manufacturers may not be able to raise this kind of capital, especially if they lose the 64K RAM market. Excluding large computer firms such as IBM and Hewlett-Packard, which produce their own semiconductors exclusively for in-house use, most U.S. semiconductor manufacturers are relatively small. The two exceptions are Texas Instruments and Motorola, with 1980 sales of $4.1 billion and $3.1 billion respectively. No other American chip company had sales of over $1 billion.

The major Japanese manufacturers by contrast are all multibillion-dollar firms, which should have little trouble raising funds. The average sales of the five largest Japanese semiconductor manufacturers in 1980 exceeded $8 billion, and the Japanese are putting this financial muscle to work. Besides investing heavily in research and development, Japanese companies are making heavy capital investments in plant and equipment.

Some of these investments will be made in Europe, where the Japanese are now trying to establish themselves. American manufacturers currently control about half of the European market, with European manufacturers accounting for most of the rest. Nippon Electric, Fujitsu, Hitachi, and Toshiba all hope to garner a significant part of this market during the 1980s. Their goal, according to a Nippon Electric spokesman, is to "push American competition from Europe." To accomplish this, Nippon Electric is currently building its second semiconductor plant in Europe, while Fujitsu and Hitachi are constructing their first European-based factories. Toshiba is also laying plans to manufacture semiconductors in Europe.

If the Japanese fail to push American companies out of Europe, the Europeans may well do it themselves. Realizing the vital importance of semiconductor technology for future industrial growth, European governments plan to spend heavily in the next five years to develop their own semiconductor industries. Their goal is to catch up with, and if possible, overtake the United States and Japan in chip-based technology. The Executive Commission of the European Economic Community (EEC) has proposed that its ten member countries coordinate their microelectronic industries by pooling research, product designs, and development. The EEC hopes to capture 30 percent of the world market by the end of the 1980s.

West German firms have already moved aggressively to acquire the latest semiconductor technology. Since 1970, West German firms have acquired either substantial or total control of five American semiconductor companies. Leading West Germany's push into semiconductors is Siemens, the electronics giant whose chip sales increased by 500 percent between 1975 and 1980. The company is already manufacturing 64K RAMs and hopes to become a major competitor in American markets by 1985. In pursuit of this goal, the company purchased Litronix, Inc., and a 20 percent interest in Advanced Micro Devices, both semiconductor firms located in Silicon Valley. These acquisitions provide Siemens with a strong technological base. To supplement these efforts, the West German government is committed to match Japanese government expenditures on semiconductor research and development.

The United Kingdom is also investing heavily in semiconductors, and the development of the industry is thought to be so important that the *Times* has termed it "The New Battle of Britain." The government is supplying $100 million to launch a major British semiconductor firm. Leading the project are a computer designer and two engineers formerly employed by Mostek Corporation, one of the most technologically advanced semiconductor manufacturers in the United States. These three have promised to deliver a world class product.

Additional semiconductor competition may be coming from the newly industrialized countries. The actual manufacturing of semiconductors is labor intensive and American companies have had manufacturing plants in developing countries since the 1960s. Eventually, these low-wage countries will be able to design and manufacture the product themselves. South Korea is already close. The South Korean government has targeted semiconductors as an essential part of its industrialization strategy. The country has recently received a loan of nearly $30 million from the World Bank to help fund the development of its own industry. Other countries will soon follow.

Faced with so many competitive threats in the 1980s, the long-term outlook for American semiconductor manufacturers is not encouraging. The Japanese have already taken the lead in the race to develop the 256K RAM, the most advanced semiconductor yet developed. Fujitsu, Hitachi, Mitsubishi Electric, and Nippon Electric have begun shipping samples of such chips.

Even more alarming is the recent news that the Japanese are on the verge of a major breakthrough to produce a chip capable of storing one million bits of information. Based on scientific tests disclosed by Nippon Electric and Toshiba in 1980, it seems likely that a one Mega bit RAM will be developed in the second half of the 1980s. This single tiny device would be capable of storing an entire unabridged English language dictionary along with an entire Japanese language dictionary. To ensure Japanese success in this endeavor, the Ministry of Trade and Technology recently announced a new $150 million government research program to assist private industry.

Such developments give credence to Charles Sporck's warning that if current trends continue, the U.S. semiconductor industry "will be overrun and destroyed within ten years." Significantly, our government seems content to sit on the sidelines while "Japan, Inc." and others move to take control of this vital industry.

8 The Watershed Industry

Although Japan's immediate objective is to gain a strong foothold in the semiconductor industry, its long-term objective is to use semiconductors as a base from which to establish itself as a world power in computers. As Jack Givens, president of Twain Associates, a consulting firm specializing in Japanese business strategy, has said, "The Japanese perceive the computer industry as the watershed competitive area of the eighties, just as steel was in the sixties. It is manifestly a Japanese national policy objective of the highest priority to become the global leader in the computer industry also. Leadership in computers, combined with the country's other competitive advantages, would virtually assure Japan's economic leadership well into the next century."

To achieve this objective, however, is another story. The Japanese face an uphill struggle. The United States has a commanding lead in computers, controlling an estimated 80 percent of the world market for large general purpose mainframe equipment. From an export point of view, computers are one of our strongest trade commodities. Our balance of trade in computers was a positive $6.4 billion in 1980.

American leadership in this $40 billion annual market stems primarily from the success of one company, International Business Machines. IBM supplies approximately two-thirds of all the general purpose mainframe computers sold in the world. In 1980, the company had worldwide sales of $26.2 billion and profits of approximately $3.6 billion. IBM's enormous size allows the company to spend over $1 billion a year on research and development. No other firm in the industry can come close to matching this. In a dynamic, fast-moving, high-technology industry such as computers, the firm with the largest R&D program has a substantial competitive advantage. IBM combines this with the cost benefits of large-scale production to remain the undisputed leader in its market. To unseat the company and, indirectly, the U.S. from this position would be an enormous task—even for "Japan, Inc."

The Japanese realize this. They have no grand illusions of overtaking IBM immediately. Instead, their strategy is to concentrate on the future. By gaining a lead over the United States in semiconductors, Japanese computer manufacturers hope to develop a new generation of computers superior to IBM's. The first part of this strategy may already have been realized. As Gene Amdahl, former chairman of the board of Amdahl Computer, pointed out in an interview in the *Harvard Business Review*: "I think the Japanese semiconductor industry is ahead of ours, not in every area, but in the areas that are the most necessary to compete."

As in the case of semiconductors, the Japanese government has taken an active role in helping to develop the computer industry. The government's involvement began in 1955 when MITI officials met with representatives of private corporations to plan for a domestic computer industry. The central element of this plan was for the government to provide financial incentives, organize research and development programs, encourage private company consolidations, and limit foreign imports through high trade barriers.

Over the next quarter century, the government contributed over $2.5 billion in seed money to spur computer development. Half of these funds were used to promote computer software, the programs which actually run the machines. A major project was the creation of the Japanese Information Processing Development Center in 1967 as a joint venture between government and private industry. Although the Japanese still trail IBM in software, they are making rapid strides with the government's help.

Another significant contribution by the government was the establishment of the Japanese Electronic Computer Corporation (JECC) to assist manufacturers in the computer leasing market. Previously, Japanese firms had lacked the financial muscle to compete in this fast-growing area. Leasing computers requires large amounts of cash since manufacturing and selling costs are incurred upfront while payments are received over an extended period of time. This problem is manageable for a company with IBM's financial base, but Japanese manufacturers lacked similar financial staying power. JECC was conceived as a financial middleman that would buy computers with funds borrowed from the government-backed Development Bank and then lease the machines.

In the early 1960s, MITI also undertook a major reorganization of the Japanese computer industry by dividing the six largest computer manufacturers into three groups of two companies each. The new groups were allowed to share their research and development activities. To keep foreign competitors at bay while these groups were gathering strength, tariffs on computers were raised from 15 to 25 percent. In addition, competitors such as IBM, which located in Japan and thus avoided these tariffs, were required to license their patents to domestic manufacturers. This made the latest American technology directly available to the Japanese and greatly speeded the industry's pace of development

Japanese computer tariffs were eventually reduced in 1975. The government continued to assist the industry, however, by following a strict "buy Japanese" policy. Even today, over 90 percent of all computer equipment used by government agencies is made by Japanese companies. Until recently, Japan's national telephone company, Nippon Telegraph and Telephone (NTT), the nation's largest user of computers and data processing equipment, bought one hundred percent of its equipment from domestic suppliers. Under pressure from the United States, NTT reluctantly agreed to open its market to international competition in 1980, but whether it will actually purchase significant amounts of U.S.-made equipment remains to be seen.

Government planning and support over the years is paying off. By the end of the 1970s, Japanese computer manufacturers controlled a majority share of their home market. Japan is the only country in the world that buys less than 50 percent of its computer equipment from American companies. In addition, Fujitsu, Ltd., has now surpassed IBM as the largest computer manufacturer in Japan, the first time that IBM has lost its market share leadership in a foreign country.

Even more importantly, Japanese manufacturers are now fully competitive in computer technology. In 1979, IBM announced the development of its 4300 line of computers to replace the company's best-selling 370 line. The 4300 offers twice the storage capacity, operates three to four times faster, uses less power, and still sells for approximately the same price as the 370. The 4300 was heralded around the world as a major technological achievement that would once again lift IBM above its competitors. Yet in a matter of months, Japanese firms were able to manufacture similar systems and price them below the 4300.

9 Flank Attacks

Control of the world computer market in coming years will be contested by Japan and the United States. Outside their home markets, European firms are not expected to be significant competitors. European technology currently lags, and it is doubtful that the gap can be narrowed in the foreseeable future. Newly industrialized countries in Asia and South America are not expected to be a factor either. Thus for the 1980s at least, the battle will be confined to just two nations. The battleground, however, will be global.

Having established a secure base in their home market, Japanese manufacturers now intend to increase overseas sales. MITI has established a goal of expanding computer exports at a rate of 30 percent a year through 1985. Manufacturers are even more ambitious and hope to increase exports at twice the rate targeted by the government.

A good proportion of Japanese exports will be directed to Southeast Asia. Because of their other trade ties, Japanese firms should fare well in the fast-growing markets of Hong Kong, Malaysia, Singapore, South Korea, and Taiwan. The Japanese are also trying to establish themselves in China, where they have already sold computer training equipment. But an increasing amount of Japanese computer exports will also flow into the United States. As the largest computer market in the world, we are an attractive target, and since the mid-1970s, Japanese manufacturers have slowly built a beachhead here from which they one day hope to launch a major assault.

Fujitsu was the first major Japanese computer manufacturer to move into the United States. It did so in 1974 by buying a 30 percent interest in Amdahl Corporation, one of two firms founded by Gene Amdahl, designer of IBM's famous 360 line of computers. Amdahl manufactures large, sophisticated computers that compete successfully against IBM. Through its stake in Amdahl, Fujitsu gained access to an invaluable technological base. Building on this base as well as on its resources in Japan, Fujitsu concluded that the time had finally come to enter the United States on its own. In 1980, the company formed a joint venture with TRW, a large American company with $4.9 billion in 1980 sales, to market Fujitsu computers. Fujitsu-TRW is predicting sales of more than $1 billion by the end of the decade.

Hitachi, Japan's second-largest computer manufacturer, entered the American market in 1978 by signing a marketing agreement with Itel Corporation of San Francisco. Itel's computer division was subsequently acquired by National Semiconductor, which is continuing to sell Hitachi equipment. Other Japanese manufacturers are also intent on establishing themselves here. Companies such as Canon, Mitsubishi, Nippon Electric, Sharp, Sony, and Toshiba all want a piece of the American market. These companies arrived at the 1981 National Computer Conference in Chicago with an impressive display of hardware. The conference left some industry experts talking about the once unimaginable possibility of a steel- or automobile-scale debacle in computers.

The American computer industry is not, however, without resources. Besides IBM, major factors in the industry include Digital Equipment with 1980 sales of $2.4 billion, Hewlett-Packard with 1980 sales of $3.1 billion, and Burroughs with 1980 sales of $4.9 billion. Smaller companies such as Prime Computer and Wang

Laboratories, both on the cutting edge of technology, are also formidable opponents.

For the moment, the Japanese are avoiding a frontal assault on these companies. As they have done elsewhere, Japanese firms are first trying to establish themselves in the least expensive end of the industry. Personal and small business computers priced from $500 to $10,000 also happen to be the fastest-growing market sector. These machines can be used to balance checkbooks, analyze investments, forecast sales, handle receivables or payroll accounts for small firms, or to play computerized games such as "Space Invaders." Sales of personal computers have soared from virtually zero in 1979 to $1.5 billion in 1981. Analysts expect the market will grow by as much as 50 percent a year through 1985 and continue at a fast pace through the end of the decade. By 1995, personal computers may be in more than half of all American homes.

At present, three relatively small American companies dominate this field. Apple Computer, a firm founded by two college drop-outs, is the market leader with about 23 percent of all sales. Tandy Corporation, owner of Radio Shack Stores, is a close second with just over 20 percent of the market. Commodore International is third with 10 percent. These companies, with limited financial war chests, could prove vulnerable to a full-scale Japanese attack. A Department of Commerce report warns that multibillion-dollar Japanese companies could capture 30 to 40 percent of personal computer sales by 1983. The seriousness of the threat is confirmed by looking at the market for inexpensive electronic cash registers—essentially very simple computers—where Japanese manufacturers have captured 50 percent of sales.

There is, however, a new American contender in the personal computer field. In August of 1981, IBM announced its first line of personal computers priced from $1,500 up to $6,000 for a fancy model with color graphics. The IBM product operates faster, has more memory capacity, and offers potentially more software than competitive equipment. It will be sold at the retail level by Sears, Roebuck and Company and by Computerland, a computer speciality store with 160 locations in the United States and Canada.

The entry of IBM into the market means that at least one American competitor has sufficient financial strength to match the big Japanese companies. Even so, some industry experts wonder whether a firm that has traditionally dealt with large industrial customers will be able to adapt itself to a consumer mass market. Indeed, Radio Shack vice president Jon Shirley has voiced more concern about the Japanese than IBM: "The Japanese are bound to be competitive. I worry about the Japanese much more than about IBM."

While the American computer industry prepares for the coming Japanese invasion in personal computers, it will also have to worry about other flank attacks in the higher-priced end of the market. In June of 1981, Fujitsu announced that it had developed the world's most powerful computer, the Falcone M383. The Fujitsu machine has the ability to store 128 million pieces of electronic data, four times the capacity of IBM's largest computer, and has a data processing speed three times faster than IBM's machine. The Japanese are also working to develop a new super computer that would be capable of operating more than fifty times faster than anything built today. The computer would be able to hear and talk like a human. To build such a machine will take all new software and hardware. The government has budgeted $150 million in supplementary research funds and has adopted a 1990 target date for this project, and even IBM will be hard pressed to match this schedule. According to an IBM spokesman, the proposed Japanese super computer is "way beyond what anybody else is talking about."

As the Japanese threat against the American computer industry gathered force, it ironically received support from the United States government. Throughout the 1970s, until the case was finally dropped in 1982, the Justice Department conducted one of the largest antitrust suits in history against IBM. The company was charged with violating Section Two of the Sherman Antitrust Act by competing unfairly to monopolize the market for general purpose digital computers. The government's proposed solution: to split IBM into ten separate companies. As Charles Sporck commented in 1979: "It is almost incomprehensible that IBM, which is probably this nation's most important industrial asset, has been under attack by the U.S. government. Can you imagine the same actions being taken in Japan?"

10 Machine Talk

In 1977 Secretary of State Cyrus Vance was on his way to Saudi Arabia to talk with Crown Prince Fahd. One topic that Vance hoped to raise with the Crown Prince was Saudi Arabia's plan to rebuild its telephone system. The Saudis' existing phone network was out of date and was to be replaced by a modern system. The Saudis had received proposals from both European and American telecommunications companies.

The winner would receive the largest telecommunications contract in history. Specifications of the project called for nearly 500,000 new telephones as well as sophisticated digital switching equipment that could be used for computer and other data communications. The contractor would be responsible for installing the equipment and maintaining it for at least five years after the new system came into operation.

Vance planned to tell the crown prince that the United States would like to see the contract awarded to one of the two American firms that had bid on the work. International Telephone & Telegraph (ITT) had submitted a proposal along with a group of American firms led by American Telephone and Telegraph (AT&T). The day before Vance was scheduled to arrive in Saudi Arabia, however, it was announced that the contract had been awarded to a consortium of European and Canadian firms led by Philips of The Netherlands, Sweden's L.M. Ericsson, and Canada's Bell Telephone. The Europeans underbid the American firms by quoting a price of $2.2

billion. AT&T's bid was $2.9 billion and ITT's was $3.4 billion.

Having lost the Saudi project, American firms were all the more determined to land the contract to rebuild Egypt's telephone system. But in 1978, when the Egyptian government reached a decision, the winners were once again Europeans. The $2 billion contract, the first stage of a $20 billion project, went to France's Thomson CSF and West Germany's Siemens. The losers were AT&T, Continental Telephone, and GTE, which had bid jointly on the project.

The American companies had not made the mistake of overbidding. This time the problem was financing and politics. The French-German consortium was able to offer the Egyptians a low-interest, government-financed loan to cover the cost of the project. The terms of the loan gave the Egyptians fifteen years to repay the principal at 5.5 percent interest, and no payments were required during the first five years. The American firms, which had to finance the project on the open market, could not come close to matching these terms.

Thomson-CSF and Siemens also recruited a political heavyweight to help their cause. A Siemens subsidiary in Austria stood to gain a sizable amount of business from the contract. Austrian Chancellor Bruno Kreisky, a close friend of Egyptian President Anwar Sadat, personally intervened in the final stage of the negotiations to help swing the deal to the Europeans.

What happened in both Saudi Arabia and Egypt calls attention to a very alarming fact: American companies are losing the global battle for control of the telecommunications industry. As *Business Week* noted early in 1980, "The world market for telecommunications is exploding. In just ten years, this $28 billion annual market will top $60 billion, and the race is on among the industrialized nations to grab as large a slice of this growing business as possible. But the U.S. industry will not be among the leaders."

The surging market in telecommunications has resulted from revolutionary developments in communications technology. Electromechanical technology, which transmits voice waves over telephone wires, is being replaced by digital technology, which changes voice waves into binary digits, speeds them to their destination, and then reassembles them into voices. Digital technology makes for better-quality and quicker transmission, is less costly, and allows computers to talk to each other directly via telephone lines.

With the advent of digital technology, countries are rushing to convert their phone systems by installing digital equipment. Demand is particularly strong among developing countries that lack their own telecommunication industries. Market stakes have risen even higher with turnkey contracts, in which the supplying firm not only provides the phones, cables, and computer switching equipment, but installs the equipment and services it as well.

The American giant, AT&T, is the largest telecommunications company in the world. Western Electric, Ma Bell's wholly owned manufacturing subsidiary, supplies nearly 25 percent of the world's telephone equipment. No other competitor has a market share of more than 15 percent. Western Electric alone had sales of $12 billion in 1980, which would have ranked the subsidiary as the twenty-second-largest corporation in America and the forty-ninth-largest in the world. Another branch of AT&T, Bell Laboratories, is one of the most respected private research facilities in the world.

AT&T's world market share reflects its near monopoly position in the United States. The company supplies approximately 90 percent of all telecommunications equipment sold here. With 180 million telephones installed—roughly eighty phones per one hundred people—the United States is by far the largest market in the world for telecommunications equipment. Japan is a distant second with fifty-one million phones. Yet despite its dominance at home, AT&T has not fared well abroad. Less than one percent of its sales come from exports.

AT&T's lack of success in foreign countries is a matter of concern. Although the United States remains the largest single market for telecommunications equipment, with approximately $15 billion in sales in 1980, the non-U.S. market is now almost twice as large. Moreover, the non-U.S. market is growing more rapidly. Unless AT&T becomes a greater force in world exports, its global market share will steadily decline. AT&T has recently formed a new subsidiary, AT&T International, to try to solve this problem.

Even ITT, long a specialist in supplying foreign markets with communications equipment, is having problems. The company, whose 1980 sales were $18.5 billion, was late in developing digital technology. It did not introduce its own digital switching equipment until the fall of 1981, long after foreign competitors were already installing digital phone systems all over the world.

AT&T and ITT face a competent and determined group of foreign competitors, the toughest of which are based in Western Europe. France's CIT-Alcatel and Thomson-CSF, The Netherlands' Philips, Sweden's L. M. Ericsson, and West Germany's Siemens are all major participants in the world telecommunications market. Unlike AT&T, they are all aggressive exporters. The three most successful are Ericsson, Siemens, and CIT-Alcatel. Ericsson has digital contracts with twenty-two different countries including Spain, Italy, and Norway. Siemens has signed contracts to install digital equipment in Argentina, Finland, Libya, and South

Africa. CIT-Alcatel, which was responsible for the world's first digital system in France in the early 1970s, has won contracts in Mexico, Sri Lanka, and Kuwait.

The Japanese are also strong in telecommunications. Nippon Electric Company (NEC), Fujitsu, Oki Electric, and Hitachi are major suppliers of digital equipment. NEC has been particularly successful. The firm recently beat out Ericsson, Philips, and Siemens to build the first part of a $4 billion digital system in Malaysia, and has also won major contracts in Argentina and Colombia. Now NEC is trying to establish itself in the American market. The company has already built two digital switching equipment factories here and hopes to become the second-largest foreign telecommunications manufacturer in the United States after Northern Telecom of Canada.

Northern Telecom, a Montreal-based firm, is the principal supplier of telecommunication equipment to Canada's Bell Telephone, but the firm is also a major factor in the U.S. market. Northern Telecom's American sales have increased from $75 million in 1975 to $900 million in 1980, and today the company has ten manufacturing and three research facilities here.

Northern Telecom's emergence as a major exporter of telecommunications equipment is directly attributable to the technological advantage the firm has gained over its American counterparts. In 1976, the Canadian firm became the first company to market a complete line of digital switching and transmission systems. One system in particular, the Digital Multiple System 10 (DMS-10), has become a bestseller in the United States, and is so superior that AT&T has signed a three-year contract to buy them from the Canadian firm.

Northern Telecom is now marketing a larger version of the DMS-10 called the DMS-100 that can handle up to 100,000 telephone lines at the same time. AT&T, GTE, and Continental Telephone have all purchased these systems.

Northern Telecom and Nippon Electric are not the only companies manufacturing telecommunications equipment in the U.S. In all, there are thirteen foreign firms located here. Furthermore, imports of communications equipment are increasing at a rapid rate after nearly doubling between 1978 and 1980.

It is not too late for AT&T to turn back this attack or, for that matter, to become an aggressive exporter of telecommunications equipment. To succeed, however, will require a determination to enter foreign markets agressively and make full use of its size and strength.

11 Voices in the Sky

One bright spot for the United States in telecommunications is satellite transmission. Next to digital technology, satellites will probably have the largest impact on the telecommunications industry of the 1980s. Satellites will speed data, dramatically cut the costs of teleconferencing, and expand television transmission.

The United States first recognized the importance of satellites in 1962, when Congress authorized the creation of the Communications Satellite Corporation (COMSAT). COMSAT was formed as a privately owned corporation to develop a global satellite communications network for the country. COMSAT's first satellite, Early Bird, was launched in 1965, and lowered the cost of a three-minute international telephone call from New York to London from $12 to $5. COMSAT has since launched satellites that are used for television transmission, weather reports, and other more technical services. The firm's revenues were nearly $300 million in 1980, and management hopes to more than triple this by the end of the decade.

COMSAT is especially hopeful about its new Satellite Business Systems (SBS), a joint venture with IBM and Aetna Life and Casualty. SBS is an all-digital satellite that provides both voice and machine communications. The first SBS satellite was launched in 1980 and another followed in 1981.

Initially, the major users of SBS will be businesses. The potential market from industry alone in the United

States is expected to be as high as $7 billion a year. SBS permits corporations to beam messages from rooftop antennas to a satellite and from there to anywhere in the world. Since SBS is an all-digital system, it allows computers to communicate directly with other computers as well as with other automated office equipment, and is 150 times faster than telephone lines. Such speed would enable an SBS user to send all of *War and Peace* across the country in just one second.

SBS will also make teleconferencing a practical reality. Teleconferencing enables executives in distant cities to see and speak with each other on video screens without ever having to leave their offices. Until recently, this form of communication had not been economical because conventional transmission facilities could not carry the video beam. Now, however, SBS will be able to direct both video and voice communications simultaneously from city to city. As a result, teleconferencing should become common in the 1980s. AT&T has already asked the Federal Communications Commission for permission to link forty-one cities with teleconferencing services. The company hopes to provide such services between Washington and New York by the end of 1981, and an additional nine cities are scheduled to be connected in 1982, with thirty more in 1983.

Satellite television broadcasting could also become a lucrative business. Signals will be beamed via satellites to home rooftop antennas shaped like dishes. In the spring of 1981, the Federal Communications Commission (FCC) gave its formal sanction to such broadcasting.

COMSAT has applied for FCC permission to market such a service. If approved, the COMSAT system will begin operating in 1985 with three channels offering a wide variety of programs. One would show major motion pictures and live concerts. A second channel would offer children's programs, the performing arts, and talk shows.

The third would concentrate on sports and adult education.

CBS and RCA (owner of NBC) have also requested FCC permission to market similar services. In addition to three new channels, CBS proposes to offer large-screen picture/stereo sound and "high-definition television" which would bring viewers a sharper, clearer picture. The RCA plan is to transmit six different channels. Three other companies have also applied for permission to embark on direct satellite broadcasting.

Satellite broadcasting would be analogous to cable television. Each subscriber would receive a small electronic unit to unscramble satellite waves and produce a picture. The service would cost households about $14 to $18 a month plus the cost of an antenna (presently about $500). This service should prove especially attractive to those areas that receive weak television signals. The National Telecommunications and Information Administration estimates there are over four million households in the United States that receive fewer than three channels and more than one million homes that receive no television signal at all. Satellite broadcasting should thus be a lucrative business.

Satellites should also be highly marketable abroad. In many developing countries, satellite communications would be far more economical than burying thousands of miles of cable.

While America is currently the leader in satellite technology, Western Europe, Japan, and even the Arab states are launching major efforts in the field. The Europeans have formed an eleven-nation consortium called the European Space Agency (ESA), and by pooling their research efforts hope one day to surpass COMSAT. ESA is scheduled to launch its first two telecommunication satellites in 1981. Independent of ESA, France and Great Britain are developing their own digital satellites to be launched in 1983.

Not to be left behind, Japan is also working feverishly to develop a digital satellite. The project is a joint venture of the Ministry of Postal Service and Telecommunications and Nippon Telephone and Telegraph. Given their expertise in microelectronics, the Japanese could become a major factor in the industry.

The Arabs also want in on the action. Sometime between 1983 and 1985, the Arab Satellite Communications Organization, comprised of twenty-one member countries, will launch a satellite built by France's Aérospatiale and Ford Aerospace & Communications. The satellite will be able to handle 17,000 telephone lines and eight television stations. The Arabs hope to have two such satellites orbiting the earth by the middle of the decade. If successful, the Arab satellites could point the way for other Third World countries intent on having their own systems. Colombia, for example, has already announced plans for a satellite.

The physical launching of all these satellites represents a market in and of itself. There are more than twenty telecommunication satellites scheduled to be launched in the United States alone between 1981 and 1985. Worldwide, the cost of satellite launches will total $1 billion by the middle of the decade.

Most of this business had been expected to go to the United States. The National Aeronautics and Space Administration (NASA) planned to utilize the space shuttle to put commercial satellites into orbit. Each shuttle launch was expected to carry two satellites. Development delays and budget cutbacks, however, have reduced the number of scheduled shuttle flights from forty-eight to thirty-four and still further cutbacks may be coming. As a result, telecommunications companies anxious to get their satellites into space are starting to look for alternatives to NASA.

A likely recipient of this business is the European Space Agency, whose Ariane Satellite launching rocket is expected to become operational in the fall of 1982. Already AT&T, the Arabs, and the Colombians have made reservations on the Ariane, and NASA officials are now worried about the possibility of a mass exodus to the ESA rocket. To hasten this process, ESA is using its government backing to offer an extremely attractive payment schedule and low interest rates, terms that NASA will not be able to match.

In the future, both the United States government and private industry should make every possible effort to maintain our present lead in satellite technology and its commercial applications. Telecommunications is such a vital technology that we simply cannot afford to fail.

Part Three

The Innovation Front

12 Science Fiction in the Factory

Science fiction fantasies of robots running factories are coming closer to reality. Robotlike machines that can weld, paint, and drill are now being used to produce automobiles, refrigerators, and other consumer goods, replacing human beings on the assembly line. Robots are even making other robots.

The appearance of robots in the labor force has resulted from tremendous advances in semiconductor technology. Machines with miniaturized circuits and memory devices are instructed to perform a variety of simple tasks. Computerized robots perform more complex operations requiring several steps and different movements. A not-too-sophisticated computerized robot can now assemble a part with as many as twenty different pieces. A more advanced robot uses its two arms to perform different jobs at the same time.

What we are witnessing is the emergence of a new phase in the industrial revolution in which machines almost completely replace human labor. Automation experts estimate that robots could eventually replace 75 percent of the current factory work force.* According to

*As recently as the fifties, such forecasts would have been accompanied by dire warnings about massive unemployment. Today, most automation experts take a different view. Although robotization could cause regional unemployment in cities such as Detroit (the United Auto Workers expects at least a 20 percent decline in membership by 1990), it is not expected to increase unemployment nationally. Partly, this is because new technologies create as well as destroy jobs. The computer industry, for example, once feared as source of unemployment, has actually generated new jobs over the past twenty years. The

forecasts by the American Society of Manufacturing Engineers and the University of Michigan, robots will be used in 5 percent of all American assembly line industries in 1982. By 1985, it is projected that robots will be performing 20 percent of the tasks currently handled by automobile workers, and by 1990, advances in robot technology should enable machines to replace humans in almost all phases of assembly line manufacturing.

General Electric hopes eventually to replace nearly half of its approximately 450,000 assembly line workers with robots. General Motors has similar plans. The reason is simple enough: replacing humans with machines can be extremely economical. A robot that performs one- or two-step tasks costs as little as $5,000, while computerized robots start at about $40,000. Highly sophisticated robots can cost $500,000 or more. But most manufacturers expect that prices will decline in the future as production volume rises and more producers enter the industry. According to estimates by Cincinnati Milacron, one of the leading robot manufacturers in the U.S., even a relatively expensive robot in the $75,000 range can achieve major savings for a company. Over a two-year period, an expensive robot working three shifts a day would cost about six dollars an hour, less than half the average cost of human labor.

The major benefit of robots is not that they are able to work faster—most have been designed to operate at human speed so they can be included in current assembly lines—but that they are more productive. A robot does not take coffee breaks, call in sick, or need vacations.

---

introduction of labor-saving technology is critical to overall economic growth, and growth is ultimately the only insurance against widespread unemployment. Moreover, because of demographic factors—the low birthrate of the 1960s and 1970s, together with declining numbers of women entering the workforce—some recent studies predict that national unemployment will fall below 3 percent by 1990, even with accelerated automation.

Robots will work twenty hours a day, including week-
ends, without overtime pay. Perhaps most importantly,
the quality of robot work is predictable and generally
free of defects.

The use of robots is not limited to assembly line industries. Robots are also useful in the small-batch production processes that account for the majority of U.S. manufacturing. It has been estimated that robots could
reduce costs by 80 percent or more in such industries.

Given the wide range of uses for robots and the money
they can save, the market for robots promises to explode
in future years. Robot sales in the United States alone
are expected to quadruple between 1980 and 1985, and
similar growth is expected in other industrialized countries. The battle to supply these markets is now developing.

Control of the robot market has profound implications
far exceeding the profit and growth potential of any single business. To a great extent, the battle for robots is the
battle for productivity, and the outcome of this struggle
will affect our ability to compete successfully in almost
all major industries—from steel and automobiles to electronics and aerospace. Robots represent a major opportunity for the United States to reverse its long slide in
productivity growth.

Just as robots represent an opportunity, however, they
also represent a potential foreign threat. The Japanese
government believes that the use of robots will double
Japanese assembly line productivity by 1985, thereby
strengthening that country's competitive position in
manufacturing industries. After touring a robot-auto-
mated automobile plant in Japan, former Secretary of
Labor William Usery remarked in amazement, "It
makes you wonder how we ever compete."

If we expect to remain competitive in such industries,
we will have to become masters of robot technology and
production. At the present time, however, the United

States is a distant second to Japan. According to the Japanese Industrial Robot Association, more than 50,000 robots were being used in Japanese factories in 1980. In sharp contrast, there were only 3,500 robots in American factories in the United States. In Japan there are nearly 150 robot manufacturers, five times as many as in the rest of the world. To date, there are only a handful of robot manufacturers in the United States. Total sales of robots in Japan reached nearly $400 million in 1980, nearly double their 1979 level, and five times what American firms sold.

The Japanese lead in robot technology as well as in production volume. Toyota Motors has begun using a robot that recognizes thirty different body styles and spray paints each car according to the specifications of the style. Robots capable of "seeing" will perform a whole new spectrum of tasks. Daniel Whitney, of Draper Laboratories, has estimated that the Japanese have at least a three-year lead on the U.S. in robotic vision.

By using the most technically advanced robots, the Japanese Ministry for International Technology and Industry hopes to have a totally automated assembly plant in operation by 1985. Fujitsu-Fanuc, Ltd., the most advanced Japanese robot maker, is already close to achieving this goal. In early 1981, the firm opened a $40 million plant in which robots manufacture other robots twenty-four hours a day with minimal help in the final stages from human employees, and the company is now working to build machines that will handle the final stages as well.

As in other areas, Japanese robot manufacturers have achieved their success with considerable support from the government. MITI invested more than $100 million during the 1970s to help develop the technology. The government also established a program of low-interest loans for small- and medium-sized companies so that they could afford to automate their operations.

There is no question that Japanese competition is more than the American robot industry can handle in its present state. Unimation, Inc., of Bethel, Connecticut, the largest manufacturer of robots in the United States, had 1980 sales of only $35 million, and its parent company, Condec Corporation, total sales of only $275 million.

Formidable competition for United States manufacturers is also developing in Europe. Bernard Chern, an analyst for the National Science Foundation, has reported that some of the best research in robotics is now taking place in West Germany and France. West Germany's Keller and Knappich is as advanced as any American firm. Siemens, a major shareholder in Fujitsu-Fanuc, Ltd., has already embarked on some joint venture activities with Fujitsu, and hopes eventually to begin manufacturing robots on its own. Renault is also moving into robotics. The firm has developed a robot which uses a TV camera for an "eye" and can identify more than 200 different parts at random and select the needed piece. Fiat is making a major effort in robotics as well. These large European firms have substantial resources to devote to robotics technology.

Faced with such potential competition, American manufacturers will either have to strengthen their product lines or become easy prey for Japanese and European companies. Japanese exports are already beginning to filter into the United States, although Japanese manufacturers are running at full capacity to meet the tremendous demand for their products at home. With Japanese domestic sales expected to increase by more than 400 percent by 1985, American manufacturers have a little breathing space, but they will eventually face even greater overseas competition.

In the long run, however, the greatest danger is not that we will lose the industry itself, but that we will fail to keep pace with the technology and thus cease to be competitive in key manufacturing industries. Such a failure could cripple our entire economy and leave us at the mercy of highly automated competitors like the Japanese and low-wage competitors in Third World countries. Already there is speculation that the Japanese government will discourage export of the latest robotic technology. By keeping the technology at home, they could build an overwhelming cost advantage in manufacturing industries. To prevent this possibility, we need a strong robotics industry of our own.

13 CAD/CAM

The factory of tomorrow will require more than industrial robots. It will also require CAD/CAM, an acronym for computer aided design and computer aided manufacturing. Together with robotics, CAD/CAM promises to make totally automated factories a reality.

Computer aided design was first developed in the 1960s at the Massachusetts Institute of Technology. MIT researchers designed software that could instruct computers to draw pictures. In the 1970s, this software was further developed to map the most sophisticated engineering designs.

Today an advanced CAD program provides both three-dimensional modeling and automatic scaling. A designer feeds a computer engineering specifications along with the shape and proportions of the component to be designed. The computer then works out the detailed calculations and displays a three-dimensional diagram of the component on a television screen. The engineer can rotate the diagram, examine it from all angles, and make improvements or adjustments. Moreover, CAD allows the engineer to test the component by electronically simulating the effects of temperature and stress.

Once a component is properly designed and the necessary data have been stored in a CAD program, CAM takes over and carries the design through the manufacturing stage. A CAM program analyzes the design data to determine how the component can best be made. The program then communicates electronically with robots, providing specific instructions on how the component is to be shaped, where holes are to be placed, and how deep to drill them. The result: complete automation.

As with robotics, the primary benefit of a CAD/CAM system is increased productivity. Experts estimate that such systems can improve productivity in the design and premanufacturing stage of a product by more than five times.

Garrett Turbine Engine Company, of Phoenix, Arizona, one of the world's leading manufacturers and exporters of small gas turbines, uses CAD/CAM to design its products and tools. The company estimates that it is saving 1,000 hours each week in design time. Parts that once took six weeks to design can now be finished in two. Lockheed Corporation has used a CAD/CAM system to reduce the time needed to redesign certain sections of airplanes by 95 percent.

CAD/CAM systems will also lead to important advances in the area of quality control. A CAM program can electronically monitor the manufacturing process to ensure that robots are not malfunctioning. The system can also test parts after they are produced to ensure they meet pre-programmed design and engineering specifications.

Given the problems experienced by our ailing manufacturing industries in production and quality control, CAD/CAM should have a very promising future. Industry sales reached $610 million in 1979, but analysts are expecting the market to explode in the 1980s. First Boston Corporation, a New York investment banking firm, predicts that sales of CAD/CAM systems will grow at an average rate of 46 percent a year through the mid-1980s. By 1990, sales could exceed $10 billion a year.

A majority of these sales should go to American companies. Small American high-technology firms such as Computervision and Calma (now a subsidiary of General

Electric) have pioneered the development of CAD/CAM and their technology remains unsurpassed. Even in Japan, 90 percent of the CAD/CAM systems sold in 1980 were supplied by American companies.

The Japanese do not, however, plan to remain dependent on the U.S. for this crucial technology. The government is currently working to help domestic companies develop their own software systems. The Ministry of International Trade and Industry allocated $60 million in 1981 alone to develop what is termed a "flexible manufacturing system," or FMS. An FMS consists of several robots working together and taking orders from a master computer. With an FMS, humans are needed only to program the master computer and to service the robots. MITI hopes to have 20 percent of Japan's manufacturing industries using such systems by the middle of the decade.

Such government-backed programs have American CAD/CAM firms worried that the Japanese will soon close the gap in this important technology. Jeff Edson, of Nicolet-CAD Corporation in San Francisco, has warned that "the Japanese certainly have the potential to become leading competitors in CAD/CAM. With heavy government support they should be able to catch up with us within three to five years." If the Japanese ever combine leadership in CAD/CAM with their robotics superiority, they will be virtually unbeatable in the basic manufacturing industries that they already dominate.

The West Germans also appear to be achieving a strong CAD/CAM capability. The Technical University of Berlin has recently developed what is considered to be the best three-dimensional modeling system in the world. German programs are considered so advanced in this area that Norway recently traded some oil exploration rights in the North Sea for access to the software.

Foreign competition is definitely catching up. If American CAD/CAM firms relax their technological pace or become too preoccupied with maximizing short-term profits at the expense of long-term market position, we could lose our advantage in this important new technology.

14 *Office of the Future*

A few years ago an executive looking for an important document might have to ask his secretary to search through hundreds of files. Today, the same task need only take a few seconds. Sitting at his desk, the executive turns to a typewriterlike keyboard, pushes a few buttons, and instantly displays the information he wants on a videoscreen.

The executive can do this and much more on a small machine, about the size of a portable television, called an executive work station. The machine is essentially a small computer with the ability to store and recall important information, automatically dial frequently used telephone numbers, and send and receive electronic messages to and from other work stations. It can be operated easily by an executive who has no knowledge of computers and only a hunt-and-peck familiarity with typing. For executives who need to work at home, there are even portable work stations that fit easily into an attaché case. These portable stations can be connected to the main-office computer via telephone.

Another major office innovation is the word processor, a machine that combines the capabilities of an electronic typewriter and a computer. Word processors allow the user to store form letters and legal documents that can later be recalled and typed automatically, saving valuable time that might otherwise be spent retyping. They also permit easy text editing by enabling the user to recall a specific paragraph on a video screen, make changes, and then reinsert the corrected paragraph back into the original text. Some machines even correct spelling errors and perform simple arithmetic.

Intelligent copiers represent another major advance in office technology. These machines communicate directly with work stations, word processors, and computers. Receiving information in digital language, an intelligent copier translates it into human language and produces a paper copy of the information. Linked by a systemwide communications network, intelligent copiers can send messages to other copiers in the same building or across the country, instructing them to produce similar copies.

Work stations, word processors, and intelligent copiers are the essential equipment around which the office of the future will revolve. Other standard options in the so-called "automated office" will be electronic mailing and filing systems. Electronic mailing systems can send memos or documents created at a work station or a word processor to any pre-programmed destination in country. To receive a message an employee simply punches in an access code on his or her work station and correspondence is automatically displayed. Such systems will allow firms to bypass the post office for much of their mail. Electronic micrographic filing systems will condense paper files by thirty to fifty times. Important documents and papers can be photographed right in the office on either microfilm or microfiche (small photographic negatives about the size of a file card on which more than 200 pages of information can be recorded) and then recalled electronically from a computerized filing system.

The key to the office of the future is to tie all these machines together so that they function as one system. The computer software to make this a reality is now being developed. Once perfected, it will drastically change office operations. A secretary who wants to arrange a meeting between busy executives in different parts of the country will only have to push a few buttons to gain access to each person's electronic calendar (stored at his or her work station). A meeting can then be scheduled at a time convenient for all. To inform each person of the meeting, the secretary will type a memo on a word processor and transmit it through an electronic mailing system. On the day of the meeting, the executives will not have to leave their offices. Instead, they will use teleconferencing facilities in their own building to see and communicate with other participants. A nearby intelligent copier will also make it possible to distribute documents during the course of the meeting.

The real benefit of the automated office is that it will improve the productivity of both the secretary and the executive. With wage rates increasing faster than productivity, and with the cost of technology decreasing, investments in automated office machinery are becoming attractive to more and more firms. The consulting firm of Booz, Allen & Hamilton has estimated that American businesses could save as much as $300 billion a year through office automation.

The potential market for automated office equipment is virtually unlimited. It has been estimated that the direct cost of office operations in 1979 exceeded $800 billion in the United States alone. On a worldwide basis, total expenditures may approach $2 trillion a year. Alan Purchase, director of business automation at Stanford Research Institute, believes that automated office equipment could be a $50-billion-a-year industry by the end of the decade. By the end of the century, the market could easily be three or four times that much.

The potential of this market has attracted some of America's largest and best-managed firms. Among the corporations hoping to obtain a sizable share of the market are IBM, Xerox, Hewlett-Packard, Texas Instruments, and even Exxon. A number of smaller firms like Wang Laboratories and Lanier Business Products also hope to carve a niche for themselves in the industry.

Although American firms pioneered much of the technology behind the office of the future, their potential competition is formidable. Some of the biggest and most successful firms in Western Europe and Japan are preparing to make major efforts in this industry.

The competition from West Germany is led by Siemens, which is already selling work stations and word processors throughout Europe. Once it establishes itself there, Siemens is likely to make the United States its next major target. Another well-known West German firm—Volkswagen—is also striving to become a major competitor in the office of the future market. The automaker hopes this business will serve as a hedge against a possible long-term decline in automobile sales. By the end of 1980, VW had spent nearly a half billion dollars acquiring the necessary technology to compete in this market. In 1979, the company acquired the West German firm Triumphwerke Nurnberg, owner of Royal Business Machines, Inc., and Adler-Royal Business Machines, Inc., both leading suppliers of office equipment. Later in the same year, VW paid $117 million to acquire Pertec Computer Corporation of Los Angeles, a producer of small-computer systems that can be used in an automated office. VW is now eyeing other acquisitions in the U.S. to complete its line of office equipment.

Olivetti, the multibillion-dollar office equipment supplier, also has hopes of capturing a major share of the office of the future market. The Italian firm manufactures a line of typewriters, word processors, and small business computers that it hopes to develop into a complete office network and sell as a package. In addition, in 1980 Olivetti entered into a joint agreement with the large French firm St. Gobain-Pont-à-Mousson to develop and market office-of-the-future equipment.

While competition from Europe is potentially threatening, it is the Japanese who are to be feared most. All the large Japanese computer companies and many of those in the consumer electronics field want to become major factors in the office automation market. Fujitsu, the leading Japanese computer manufacturer, has assembled all the necessary technology for the office of the future. The firm is manufacturing work stations, word processors, and laser printers, as well as developing the software necessary to interconnect all these machines. Fujitsu has already begun its assault on the American market. In 1980 the firm acquired DPF Leasing, developer of a high-powered word processing machine with electronic mail and document storage features. Fujitsu is completing the machine, called The Word Machine, and hopes to introduce it sometime in 1982.

Sony, which is trying to diversify beyond consumer electronics, is planning a major effort in office equipment. In late 1980, the company dazzled the industry by announcing the development of two new word processors with unique capabilities. Both machines—one a stand-alone unit and the other a portable—come equipped with a microcassette recorder for dictation and voice storage. Sony was also able to improve the file capacity of the disc memories used in its word processors. Its machines store the same amount of information on a three-and-one-half-inch-diameter disc that competitors get on a five-and-one-half-inch disc. Furthermore, the stand-alone unit contains a full-page video display that simulates the appearance of black type on white paper to show the user what the page will look like before it is printed. These two machines are only the beginning. Sony has plans to introduce other automated office equipment in the near future.

Matsushita, Hitachi, Nippon Electric, Oki Electric, Rioch, Sharp, Mitsubishi, and Toshiba are all preparing to enter the fight as well. Each hopes to acquire some part of the market. While total production of word processors in Japan was only $25 million in 1980, the Japan Office Machinery Association estimates that this will increase to $100 million by 1985 and $500 million by 1990. The association further expects that Japan will be exporting more than $100 million in word processors by the end of the decade.

An indication of potential Japanese strength in the office-of-the-future market can be seen in the present battle for plain-paper office copiers. American firms such as Xerox, IBM, and Kodak have long reigned supreme in this market, where U.S. sales alone are nearly $12 billion a year. Xerox, with $8 billion in sales in 1980, has been so successful that its name has become synonymous with copying machines. In recent years, however, the firm has begun to lose its once dominant position. Dataquest, a California-based market research organization, estimates that Xerox held 85 percent of the U.S. market for copy machines at the beginning of the 1970s; by 1980, it was just over 50 percent and declining.

Xerox has retreated in the face of aggressive Japanese pricing tactics. Led by Ricoh and Canon, the Japanese broke into the market by selling small, efficient copying machines that cost thousands of dollars less than Xerox products. In the mid-1970s, the cheapest Xerox machine sold for $19,000 while some Japanese models sold for less than $5,000. Xerox machines offered greater speed, but the extra fraction-of-a-second per copy saved was not worth the additional expense to many customers. Exploiting this opening, the Japanese attacked relentlessly. Of the more than 250,000 low-priced plain-paper copiers sold in the United States in 1979, nearly 175,000 were made by Japanese companies.

The largest Japanese exporter of copiers, Ricoh, dominates the low-priced end of the market. It has captured more than 40 percent of plain-paper copier sales in Japan and 35 percent of sales here. Its 1980 worldwide sales topped $1 billion. Until 1981, however, Ricoh machines were sold in the United States under the Savin name.

Now Ricoh wants to establish its own name and is gearing up to make a major effort beginning in 1983. The company has already built a production facility in California capable of producing 5,000 copiers a month.

Canon, the world's largest manufacturer of cameras, is also a leading innovator in copiers. More than half of the plain-paper copiers sold in the world in 1979 were based, at least in part, on technology pioneered by Canon. The firm's sales in the United States have increased from $6 million in 1975 to $140 million in 1980, and Canon hopes to continue this rapid growth with a new machine introduced in 1980. Using such advanced technologies as microelectronics and fiber optics, Canon developed a small desktop copier called the NP-200, which makes as many as twenty copies a second, is mechanically reliable, simple to repair, and costs less than $3,500.

Twelve other Japanese companies are now selling copiers here as well. As a result, competition at the lower-price end of the market has become intense. One major U.S. manufacturer has already abandoned the copier market—in 1981, no less formidable a competitor than IBM announced that it was going to buy desktop copiers from Minolta and sell them under the IBM name.

Having established their dominance in low-priced copiers, the Japanese are now preparing to attack the higher-priced, higher-profit end of the market. As in the past, they will try to establish themselves by offering machines better or equal in quality at prices 20 percent or more below those of Xerox, IBM, or Kodak. Canon has developed a super fast copier that produces 135 copies a minute, fifteen more copies per minute than Xerox's fastest machine and sixty more than IBM's fastest model. Ricoh is marketing an intelligent copier that is based on laser technology and is capable of drawing graphs from electronically fed data. Other Japanese competitors will undoubtedly follow Canon and Ricoh into the high-priced end of the market. Consequently, Xerox will find itself even harder pressed to maintain its market share in the 1980s.

The plain-paper-copier struggle is the first major skirmish in the battle to win control of the $100 billion office-of-the-future market. By seizing the low-priced end of the market, the Japanese have won a place for themselves in office equipment. If they gain significant market share in the high-priced end of the copier market as well, they will be well positioned to win control of the entire office-of-the-future market.

15 Genetic Engineering

Genetic engineering is one of the most important scientific developments of this century. The most advanced state of the art centers around recombinant DNA (deoxyribonucleic acid). Basically, genetic engineering involves splitting genes and grafting genetic material from one organism to another, a process that can be used to create entirely new organisms with capabilities not found in nature. Using such techniques, scientists are making dramatic breakthroughs that potentially affect a wide range of industries.

The most publicized developments have been in medicine. In early 1980, Biogen, a Swiss-based firm, announced that it had genetically constructed interferon, a possible weapon against everything from the common cold to cancer. In actuality, however, little is known about the curative or preventive powers of interferon since so little of it has been available for scientific testing. Previously, the only way to obtain the substance was to extract it from human blood, and it required enormous quantities of blood to produce the tiniest amount of interferon—6.5 million pints of blood to produce just one ounce. As a result, the substance has been astronomically expensive. According to the American Cancer Society, one pound of pure interferon produced using current techniques would be worth more than $20 billion. Through genetic engineering, it may now be possible to make large quantities at reasonable prices.

The other major breakthrough in the medical field has been the production of human insulin by Genentech, a

San Francisco-based genetic engineering firm. In the past, the only way to obtain human insulin had been to extract it from cadavers. This is not a feasible means of obtaining the mass quantities of insulin necessary to supply the more than one and a half million diabetics who live in this country alone. Instead, the insulin used by diabetics has to be obtained from the pancreases of slaughtered pigs and cows. Possible negative long-term side effects of using animal insulin, however, make it much less desirable than human insulin. Thanks to genetic engineering, human insulin should be available in mass quantities by the end of the decade.

Genetic engineering has also created some promising new vaccines. Scientists are hopeful of using gene splicing techniques to develop new vaccines for dysentery, hepatitis, and malaria, and genetic engineers have already produced a potential vaccine against the deadly killer of cattle and sheep, hoof-and-mouth disease.

Although medical applications of genetic engineering receive the most publicity, the most immediate uses of the new science are in agriculture. Scientists expect to obtain major improvements in both the yield and nutritional content of crops. Genetic engineering should also lead to crops that are more resistant to disease and able to live for long periods without water.

One way scientists are trying to improve crop yields is by increasing the efficiency of photosynthesis, the process whereby plants convert sunlight into food energy. Currently plants are able to convert only one percent of the sunlight they absorb. Genetic researchers hope to improve on this percentage. If plants can be genetically manipulated to convert 2 percent, it would double their rate of growth and dramatically increase the world's food supply.

Important research is also under way to increase the protein content of crops such as corn. By altering the crop's gene structure, scientists may be able to increase its ability to store protein and thus make corn more nutritious for human as well as animal consumption. If they succeed in this effort—and early indications appear favorable—it could provide a big boost to American farmers—the world's largest producers of corn.

Scientists hope to be able to apply similar genetic techniques to animals. It should be feasible to combine desirable genetic traits to create bigger and healthier livestock. Breakthroughs are already being made, and the president of one leading genetic firm predicts that by the end of the century scientists will be able to produce animals to specified designs.

Genetic engineering also has applications in the chemical industry. Enzymes have been created that speed chemical reactions more than one million times. Cetus Corporation of San Francisco, a firm founded in 1971 to pursue commercial applications of genetic engineering, has developed new ways of producing petrochemicals at costs already comparable to existing techniques.

Applications of genetic engineering are virtually unlimited, and given the importance of this new technology, it is imperative that the United States remain at the forefront. However, we are currently locked in a three-way race with Western Europe and Japan for leadership.

We appear to be ahead in applying genetic engineering to agriculture. In the medical and pharmaceutical field we are about even with Western Europe. Genentech and the Indianapolis-based pharmaceutical manufacturer Eli Lilly have a slight lead in the race to produce human insulin, but the large French chemical company Rhône-Poulenc is right behind. Two Swiss companies, Hoffman-La Roche and Biogen, lead in the manufacture of interferon, with American and Japanese companies close behind. In chemicals, we face a stiff challenge from the Japanese, who lead the world in use of fermentation techniques to produce chemicals, antibiotics, and food products. Japan secured over 66 percent of world patents in this area between 1977 and 1980, more than three times the U.S. share. Although the United States seems to have a slight advantage in the genetic engineering of enzymes to speed fermentation, the Japanese are better able to put the technology to work.

For the moment, then, we appear to be well positioned in all areas of biotechnology. But our lead is tenuous at best. In a year or two, Japan or any of the major Western European countries could pass us by and move to the forefront of this exciting new science. The governments of Japan, West Germany, France, and the United Kingdom are all funneling money to private industry to accomplish this objective.

The Japanese government has identified genetic engineering as an especially high priority area. As in the case of other key high-technology industries, the government plans to play an active role in promoting the development of the field. The Ministry of International Trade and Industry is organizing a ten-year $150 million effort to pursue advances in biotechnology. To supplement this program, the five leading Japanese chemical companies have established a joint research association. The government is directly involved in the development of commercial applications for the technology as well. It has provided $4 million to each of two leading pharmaceutical companies to aid them in their quest to mass produce interferon.

The European Economic Commission is proposing to fund a five-year $50 million joint research program designed to move Europe to the forefront of genetic engineering technology. This will be in addition to the efforts of each member country.

The French consider genetic engineering to be one of the "locomotive technologies" that will pull France through the 1980s, and their government has established a research unit called the Groupe Génie Génétique (G3) to pursue advances in the science. G3 has already developed a promising vaccine against hepatitis.

In West Germany, home of the world's three largest chemical companies, BASF, Bayer, and Hoechst, each of the firms has an active genetic engineering program. To support these efforts, the government is spending heavily on basic research. In 1980, over $20 million was allocated for such efforts. Part of this money goes to support the Gesellschaft für Biotechnologische-Forschung, the only research institute in Europe entirely devoted to genetic engineering.

The British government is also getting into gene splicing by helping fund a company called Celltech, which will pursue various research and commercial applications in the field.

Not only are foreign firms receiving the benefit of government-financed research, they also are gaining access to the latest American research in biotechnology. Hoffman-La Roche established an institute for molecular biology in New Jersey as far back as 1967. The institute, which now employs over one hundred researchers, contracts with leading American scientists to serve as visiting lecturers. Biogen has hired many prominent American scientists, including Walter Gilbert, a 1980 Nobel Prize winner. Hoechst has underwritten a $50 million research grant for work in genetic engineering by Massachusetts General Hospital, one of the working hospitals of Harvard Medical School, and has been guaranteed patent rights on any developments stemming from the grant as well as the right to send scientists to Mass General for training.

Thus armed with the latest American scientific knowledge and the financial backing of their governments, Western European and Japanese firms should prove to be tough competitors. The question remains whether upstart American companies like Genentech and Cetus Corporation will be able to stay at the forefront of this critical industry.

16 Alternatives to OPEC

In the 1970s, OPEC nations became a major economic and political force by controlling critical supplies of international oil, and they should retain much of this power for the rest of the century at least, since oil is expected to remain the world's primary source of energy.

Over the next twenty years, however, OPEC will not be able to supply enough oil to meet all the world's energy needs. According to Exxon's "World Energy Outlook Report of 1980," world demand will increase 65 percent by the end of the century, but only a slight increase in production is expected. As a result, a barrel of oil may cost more than $400 by the year 2000, according to one Department of Energy estimate.

At these prices, countries are going to have to look for alternative ways to supply their energy needs. Exxon expects that oil will account for only 30 percent of the world's energy consumption by the end of the century versus 50 percent now, so nations able to supply alternative energy will, like OPEC, be assured of international economic and political power.

In the immediate future, coal offers an obvious alternative to oil. Coal is abundant—there are enough reserves to provide energy for at least the next one hundred years—and it is still relatively inexpensive. As oil prices continue to rise, more and more manufacturers and utilities will convert from oil to coal. As a result, Exxon estimates that world demand for coal will grow 3 percent a year over the next twenty years compared to less than one percent a year for oil. By the year 2000, coal should rival oil as the primary source of world energy.

A coal boom could benefit the American balance of trade. Approximately one-third of world coal reserves are located here. Coal exports, which totaled $4.5 billion in 1980, are expected to have a real (inflation adjusted) growth rate of 5 percent a year over the next twenty years.

Although we appear well positioned to benefit from a shift to coal, a number of factors could work against us. In particular, the cost of mining and transporting coal within our country could put us at a cost disadvantage relative to other major coal exporting nations such as Poland, Australia, and the Soviet Union. American coal miners are already among the highest paid in the world. Taking into account production bonuses, they can earn more than $30,000 a year, or double what they earned a decade ago.

Unfortunately, productivity has not kept pace with such wage increases. During the 1970s productivity increased by just 20 percent. One reason for this is the number of days lost to wildcat strikes. The United Mine Workers Union has long been one of the nation's most militant unions. Virtually any labor dispute can shut down a mine—Merrill Lynch estimates that during the 1970s the coal industry lost nearly ten million worker days to wildcat strikes.

Increasing rail rates also threaten to put American coal at a cost disadvantage. Nearly 70 percent of all coal mined here is transported by rail. The cost of moving this coal doubled during the last decade. In the late 1970s, the city of San Antonio, Texas, claimed that the rates charged for transporting coal from Wyoming were so high that it was cheaper to buy coal from Australia and have it shipped to the Texas Gulf.

A further problem is that an increasing proportion of

the nation's coal will be mined in the Western states, where our rail system is not extensive. Western states now provide less than 30 percent of the nation's coal, but this is expected to increase to 50 percent by the end of the century. Western coal is more accessible to surface mining, is much cleaner to burn, and will be in strong demand by Western utilities. Whether Western railroads will be able to handle all the traffic created by this increased demand is highly questionable.

East Coast coal producers suffer from transportation handicaps of another sort. Port facilities for shipping coal are so poor that we have not been able to keep up with export demand. In 1980, coal-carrying ships had to wait as long as sixty days in some harbors to pick up cargo. These delays can increase shipping costs by as much as $15,000 a day. As a result, some potential customers have sought coal elsewhere.

It is estimated that the coal industry lost $500 million in export sales in 1980 because of the port situation. Efforts are now under way to improve port facilities for shipping coal, but this could prove to be a long and frustrating process. In 1970, the city of Baltimore decided to deepen its port channel by an additional ten feet so that larger ships, including big coal vessels, could use the port. Because of an environmental battle over where to dump the dredge from digging, the city did not receive permission to deepen the harbor until 1980.

Even if we are able to solve our transportation problems and keep our labor costs in line, other obstacles will remain. There are still serious environmental concerns about mining and burning coal which must be overcome. Workers in underground mines risk black lung disease. Surface, or "strip" mining, which involves digging large holes and stripping coal from each side, has serious environmental side effects. Of still greater concern are the pollution problems of burning coal, including the release of carbon dioxide into the atmosphere.

For these reasons and others, many energy experts consider coal to be a "transition fuel" while alternative energy sources are being sought. Synthetic fuels, solar energy, and fusion are all promising high-technology alternatives to traditional fossil fuels. The countries that first successfully develop these technologies will be able to export their expertise all over the world. Despite the huge potential payoff for pioneering these technologies, the United States is not doing enough to ensure that it will be among the leaders in alternative energy.

"Synthetic fuels" is a generic term that refers to the production of oil and natural-gas substitutes from other feedstocks. Specific technologies include oil shale, coal liquefaction, coal gasification, and tar sands. Synthetic fuel facilities could produce as much as 8 percent of the world's energy supply by 2000.

Oil shale is potentially the most promising synthetic fuel. It is derived from a fine-grained rock called marlstone, which contains large amounts of an organic substance called kerogen. When heated to very high temperatures, kerogen separates into oil and other byproducts. According to the U.S. Geological Survey, more than two quadrillion barrels of oil could be recovered from shale worldwide. (A quadrillion is a 1 followed by 15 zeros.) Some of the world's richest oil shale deposits are to be found in Colorado, Utah, and Wyoming. In total, it is estimated that we have enough shale reserves to produce 200 trillion barrels of oil.

Despite the enormous potential of oil shale and other synthetic fuels, the United States is taking a very cautious approach to developing this technology. To date no commercial-scale synthetic fuel plants have been built—although several are now in the early construction stage.

The United States Synthetic Fuels Corporation, created by the government in 1980 to spur the development of the industry, has accomplished little so far. The corporation was initially authorized to provide loan guarantees, price supports, purchase commitments, direct loans, and joint ventures for synthetic fuel projects. The Reagan Administration has not, however, shown a great deal of enthusiasm for spending public monies to subsidize the development of the industry, and the new chairman of the corporation has already told Congress that he will proceed more slowly than expected. While we debate the merits of the technology, Australia, Brazil, Canada, China, Japan, the Soviet Union, and West Germany are developing synthetic fuel industries of their own.

A potentially better source of energy is the sun. Solar energy could provide a free and endless supply of power if we could learn to convert and store this energy efficiently. Although full-scale commercial use is still some years off, rapid progress is being made, and solar energy now heats more than 100,000 American homes. The Energy Project of the Harvard Business School has estimated that solar energy could supply 20 percent of the nation's energy needs by the end of the century.

One of the keys to the future development of solar energy is the photovoltaic cell—a tiny silicon wafer that absorbs sunlight and converts it into electricity. In 1977, the cost of these cells was a prohibitive $50 per watt of electricity generated. By 1981, the cost had fallen to less than $6 per watt. The Department of Energy expects that future cost-reductions will bring the price below $1 per watt by 1986, at which time solar energy should start to become cost competitive with other forms of energy. When this occurs, the design and manufacturing of photovoltaic cells will become a major growth business. Industry analysts estimate that photovoltaic-cell sales will increase from $5 million in 1980 to $5 billion by the end of the decade.

American companies lead the world in solar technology, but the Japanese are strong challengers. Beginning with the Sunshine Project, launched by the Ministry of

International Trade and Industry in 1974 to find a solution to the country's energy problems, the government has been helping to finance the development of solar energy. The Japanese achieved a first in 1981 by generating 1,000 kilowatts of electricity from a solar energy plant. MITI has even bigger things in mind, including a photovoltaic cell with the capacity to generate electricity for less than fifty cents per watt. If a joint Japanese business-government research program succeeds in developing such a cell, Japan could assume technological leadership of the industry. Despite this threat, the Reagan Administration has made substantial cutbacks in government-funded solar energy programs.

Fusion may be the ultimate solution to the world's energy problems. Fusion is the type of nuclear reaction that powers the sun and the hydrogen bomb. Harnessing fusion would provide an endless supply of cheap, safe energy. Fusion is the opposite of fission, the process that powers nuclear energy plants. Fission involves splitting the center of a uranium atom, thereby releasing an enormous amount of energy. Fusion, on the other hand, involves bonding together the nuclei of two hydrogen atoms to create helium. This process frees an extra neutron and creates energy. An important advantage of fusion is that there is no possibility of a major nuclear accident occurring such as the core meltdown that was narrowly avoided at Three Mile Island.

The technology behind fusion is much more complex than that for fission. To fuse hydrogen atoms together requires tremendous heat. The most promising approach for producing a fusion reaction requires that hydrogen be heated to 80 million degrees—five times hotter than the surface of the sun. Understandably the technology needed to produce such temperatures in a confined environment is extremely complicated. Yet scientists at Princeton University, where some of the most advanced fusion research in the world is taking place, hope to be able to produce a fusion reaction by the end of this decade. Even if this happens, building a fusion reactor to produce electricity is still many years away.

The Soviet Union and Japan and Western Europe are all aggressively proceeding with fusion research and development. The Soviets pioneered much of the early fusion research and may be the first to harness fusion for commercial use. The Japanese, building on the work of both the U.S. and the U.S.S.R., are now beginning to make progress under the direction of their own government-funded research program. Western European countries have banded together in a joint effort to advance fusion technology.

If we are to avoid falling behind the competition, we will have to act now. In 1980, the House of Representatives passed a bill that allocated $20 billion to build a demonstration reactor by the end of the decade. This supplemented a limited Department of Energy fusion research budget. The Senate deleted all funds from the bill and extended the date for construction of the demonstration fusion facility to the end of the century. By then, the Soviets and the Japanese may have assumed leadership of this technology.

The United States seems well positioned to become a leading player—if not the leading player—in new energy technologies, for our rich natural resource base and our technological expertise in the energy field give us an advantage over foreign competition. But our advantage is slight. The competition is pouring billions of dollars into national energy plans to develop alternative fuels, while we still lack a coherent energy policy. The Reagan Administration's answer is essentially to leave the development of alternative forms of energy to the free market, but the danger of this strategy is that American companies may not have the resources or the long-term outlook needed to succeed in this vital industry.

17 American Ingenuity

Robotics, CAD/CAM, the automated office, genetic engineering, and alternative energy sources are a few of the high technologies around which the global battle for industrial supremacy will center. In coming years, entirely new technologies will also emerge, the result of scientific breakthroughs made in this decade and the next.

America has long been the world leader in technological and scientific innovation. The light bulb, telephone, airplane, semiconductor, and computer are well-known examples of American ingenuity, and such technological innovation has played a fundamental role in our emergence as the world's leading economic power. The Department of Commerce has estimated that technological innovation was directly responsible for 45 percent of our economic growth between 1929 and 1969.

Technological innovation contributes to economic growth in two important ways. First, new machines and new industrial processes increase productivity and lower the cost of manufacturing existing products. Second, new products and industries are created that did not exist in the past. Both of these processes are essential to industrial success.

Technological innovation is especially important in industrialized countries that must constantly innovate to maintain a comparative advantage over low-wage competitors. As Princeton University professor Robert Gilpin noted in a report prepared for the Joint Economic

Committee of Congress, ". . . a high-wage economy, such as that of the United States, in a world where new knowledge and technological innovation rapidly diffuses to lower-wage economies, must be able to innovate and adopt new technologies with equal rapidity if it is to remain competitive. American firms must in fact run faster and faster merely to stand still."

American firms are not, however, running faster. American investment in research and development as a percentage of gross national product declined during the 1970s. In the 1960s, our R&D expenditures averaged 2.8 percent of GNP. In the 1970s, this average fell to 2.4. By 1980 we were spending just 2.3 percent of GNP on R&D activities. During the same period, West Germany's expenditures on R&D as a percent of gross national product increased by nearly 100 percent, the Soviet Union's by 33 percent, and Japan's by 20 percent.

In 1960, we were spending a higher percentage of our GNP on research and development than any other country in the world. By 1978, we trailed both the Soviet Union and West Germany. According to the National Science Foundation, the figures for 1978 were:

Country	*R&D/GNP%*
Soviet Union	3.47
West Germany	2.31
U.S.A.	2.24
United Kingdom	2.13
Japan	1.93
France	1.76

These figures are somewhat misleading, however, since defense-related expenditures are included. The U.S. spends more on military R&D than any other nation, with the possible exception of the Soviet Union. Although technology developed for defense purposes can sometimes be applied to other industries, much of it is specialized.

The crucial element in the battle for industrial supremacy is expenditure on industrial research and development. If one looks solely at these expenditures, the facts are not reassuring. In the 1970s, American companies spent an average yearly total of 1.5 percent of GNP on industrial research. This trailed both West Germany and Japan, which averaged 2.0 percent and 1.9 percent of GNP respectively. Data on the Soviet Union is not available because a distinction between government and business expenditures cannot be made.

It is not altogether clear why our investment in industrial R & D is declining. One likely answer is that American managers are too short-term oriented to invest for the long-term payoff of basic research. Another possible explanation is that money that was previously being spent on R & D is now being used to comply with government regulations enacted in the 1970s. Chase Manhattan Bank estimates American businesses are spending more than $100 billion a year to comply with government regulations. According to Rawleigh Warner, Jr., chairman of the board of Mobil Oil, "Industry has been compelled to spend more of its research dollars to comply with environmental, health and safety regulations—and to move away from longer-term efforts aimed at major scientific advance."*

The real reason for our declining commitment to R&D is probably some combination of these two explanations. But whatever the cause, the implications of our

---

*Companies could of course increase R&D budgets to accommodate both regulatory compliance and traditional activities. Many pressures weigh against this, however—particularly while inflation squeezes corporate cash flow and profits in real (inflation adjusted) terms.

lagging commitment to R&D are clear: productivity growth has slowed and American ingenuity is on the decline.

Productivity growth in the United States in the 1970s was dismal. Japan and most of the Western European nations surpassed us by a ratio of two to one. The productivity of American workers was actually greater in 1978 than in 1979.

New-product innovation has also been retarded by R&D cutbacks. Both the absolute and relative number of patents issued to American firms on first-of-a-kind inventions declined in the 1970s. The share of U.S.-issued patents to Americans fell from 78 percent in 1967 to 63 in 1977. During the same period, Japan's share of U.S.-issued patents increased from 2 to 10 percent; and West Germany's from 6 to 8 percent. The number of foreign patents issued to American companies also declined between 1966 and 1976. In a ten-country survey, which included West Germany, Japan, the United Kingdom, and Canada, the number of patents issued to American firms declined almost 30 percent.

Furthermore, according to a study by the Stanford Research Institute, our share of major scientific and technological innovations has fallen. In the 1950s, the United States initiated over 80 percent of the world's major innovations; today it is closer to 50. Meanwhile, the relative number of major innovations attributable to West Germany, France, and Japan has been increasing.

Our slipping commitment to research and development has serious implications for our future. If the United States becomes a technological follower, we will lose a vital edge we held over economic competitors. The result will be slower economic growth and a gradual loss of world economic power.

To avoid this, we must begin taking action now to reverse the trends of the 1970s. We have the human resources to restore American ingenuity to its former place as well as more Nobel prizewinners than the rest of the world combined.

The outlook, however, is not favorable. The National Science Foundation predicts that expenditures on R&D in the United States will decline further to 2.0 percent of GNP by 1985. The National Resource Council, in a report on future innovations in science and technology published in 1981, warned that "a number of proposed initatives for industrial innovation have been severely curtailed. While there seems to be a commitment in principle to keep U.S. industry at the leading edge of R&D, such cuts . . . do not promote an optimistic view."

Part Four

Friends and Adversaries

18 MOF and MITI

When the allied occupation ended in 1952, Japan's economic prospects were bleak. Industry had yet to recover from the destruction of World War Two. The country had few natural resources—nearly all of its oil had to be imported—and mountainous terrain made two-thirds of a land base smaller than Montana virtually unusable for industrial or agricultural purposes.

By the 1980s, however, Japan had emerged as an industrial giant, with a gross national product that ranks third in the world after the United States and the Soviet Union. Japanese firms have established leadership in steel, automobiles, and consumer electronics and are now bidding to dominate high-technology industries.

Japan's current economic success is visible on several levels. Unemployment is almost nonexistent, productivity growth is the highest in the world, and inflation averaged just 5 percent a year from 1975 to 1980. Average Japanese wages are well above those of the British and the French and are nearly equal to those in the United States, except in such industries as steel and automobiles.

Japan is now America's leading economic competitor and seems to be gaining on us year by year. The United States has run a trade deficit with Japan every year since 1966. Over the last decade, this deficit totaled $47.1 billion, and in 1980 alone, it reached nearly $10 billion.

Some leading economic experts believe that Japan has already surpassed us as an industrial power. According to Harvard Professor Ezra Vogel, author of the international bestseller *Japan as Number One*, "the extent of Japanese superiority over the United States in industrial competitiveness is underpublicized in America, but the true state of affairs was reflected by a high official of a leading Japanese research center who privately acknowledged that the United States with its highly competitive agricultural sector has by now taken the place of Japan's prewar colonies, supplying agricultural products and raw materials to superior modern industrial nations."

Much has been written about the reasons for Japan's success. Books analyzing the Japanese management style extoll "participatory management" and "management by consensus." Others say that the key lies in a unique cultural environment that has molded a nation of zealots dedicated to advancing their companies and country. These factors all contributed to Japan's success, no doubt, but they are not the whole story.

Some Americans charge that the Japanese have succeeded by using unfair trade practices to gain entry into our markets. Although there was justification for this claim in the past, the Japanese are now competing as fairly and openly as any other country. Other critics suggest that Japan is shutting our goods out of their markets with tariffs and with more subtle nontariff barriers such as onerous reporting and testing requirements. This claim is clearly untrue in the area of tariffs, for Japanese official barriers today are about equal to those maintained by the United States, and as a result of the Tokyo Round of Trade Agreements, Japan's average tariff rate will be 25 percent below ours by 1987. Although nontariff barriers are still a problem, they have also been greatly reduced in recent years and do not explain the low volume of American exports to Japan.

To understand Japan's success without resorting to folk tales and alibis, one must start with the pivotal role played by their government in directing the economy.

Although most major Japanese companies are private, the government has a powerful influence on the structure and actions of business, and not only tries to identify business areas in which Japan can excel, but also strives to promote and develop them.

At the heart of this system are the two most powerful agencies, the Ministry of Finance (MOF) and the Ministry of International Trade and Industry (MITI), staffed by the brightest graduates of the Japanese educational system—in sharp contrast to the United States, where the top graduates from the best business and law schools shun the public sector for more lucrative jobs in the private sector. In Japan, the highest-ranking graduates from the leading universities (of which Tokyo University is considered the best) compete fiercely for government jobs. In the most prestigious ministries—such as MOF and MITI—there are more than fifty applicants for every opening, and successful applicants must pass a written examination as well as a rigorous set of interviews.

The single most powerful government agency is the Ministry of Finance, which sets the yearly budget for all other agencies. While not directly involved with the private sector, it asserts a powerful influence over business through tax credits, direct grants, and industry subsidies. Additionally, through its influence on Japan's banking system, MOF has an indirect but significant voice in choosing industries and firms that will receive loans and the terms on which they will be made. Industries thought to be vital to the continued economic growth of the country can count on receiving all the financial support they need.

The Ministry of International Trade and Industry is even more directly involved in shaping industrial policy, and assumes the role of "strategic planner" for the economy. The ministry's avowed purpose is to strengthen

Japan's competitive position in the world economy, and in pursuit of this goal, intervenes in the marketplace when necessary to promote a more efficient use of resources.

The key concepts around which MITI shapes policy are industrial specialization and market dominance. In the 1950s, when Japan was still a low-wage country, MITI sought to encourage the development of industries such as steel, automobiles, and consumer electronics, but now that Japan is a high-wage country, the agency hopes to position Japan primarily in high-technology sectors.

MOF and MITI display little sympathy for declining industries. The government attempts to shift vital economic resources out of declining industries and into growing ones as quickly and as efficiently as possible. MITI tries to anticipate industrial decline before it happens rather than waiting until trouble has arrived and protectionist pressures have mounted. If they determine that an industry can no longer remain competitive on a world level, the government will encourage and even assist companies to go out of business.

Textiles are a case in point. Realizing that the industry was losing its comparative advantage to low-wage competitors, the government offered the least efficient companies a series of tax incentives to scrap their old weaving machines and close down. During the period from 1972 to 1978, the number of firms in the industry was reduced from 121,000 to 10,000, and only the largest and most modern survived. Today Japan's textile exports are once again booming.

When such structural adjustments are deemed necessary, MITI works closely with industry to establish programs for displaced workers, and offers tax incentives to strong industries willing to build new factories in areas with plant closings. The agency also encourages the consolidation of important industries in order to gain economies of scale. Antitrust laws are waived where necessary.

Industry executives need not follow government suggestions. The automobile industry ignored MITI's suggestions to merge and went on to become an international success anyway. More characteristic, however, was MITI's effectiveness in encouraging shared research and development in the semiconductor and computer industries.

MITI's grand plan for the Japanese economy is laid out in a report entitled "The Vision of MITI Policies in the 1980s." The report identifies semiconductors, computers, robots, and telecommunications as specific areas that are vital to Japan's continued economic prosperity. With respect to "epoch-making technological innovations," MITI thinks Japan is capable of creating breakthroughs in biogenetics, alternative energy sources, and data processing.

To succeed with its high-technology strategy, Japan will have to make the transition from a copier to an innovator. As the MITI report points out: "In the past [our] industry achieved brilliant results in improving and applying imported technologies. In the 1980s, however, it will be essential for Japan to develop technologies of its own."

The MITI plan is primarily defensive and will require significant expenditures on research and development. But Japanese industry has no other choice. The nation's economic performance over the past twenty years has been spurred by successes in such basic industries as shipbuilding, steel, automobiles, and consumer electronics. In the 1980s, however, Japan is going to be increasingly hard pressed to maintain its advantage in these areas.

Newly industrialized countries such as Taiwan, Hong Kong, and South Korea are emerging as strong competitors in a wide spectrum of basic industries. Having mastered the technology needed to manufacture radios, televisions, and even steel, the NICs are attempting to exploit their low-cost labor advantage to gain a competitive edge in these industries. In effect, the NICs will try to do to Japan what the Japanese did to us.

This is already beginning to happen. Taiwan, Hong Kong, and Singapore are gaining share in consumer electronics, and in steel, the first signs of Japan's decline are evident. Experts predict that even the automobile market will eventually be assaulted by NICs.

Both business and government in Japan realize the seriousness of this threat, and Japanese industries are striving to automate as quickly as possible to offset their growing disadvantage in labor costs. As we have seen, that nation already leads the world in the use of industrial robots. At the same time, business is planning to move offshore those labor-intensive manufacturing industries that are less susceptible to automation. For some years, Japanese companies have been investing in television and textile plants abroad, especially in Malaysia and Taiwan; now MITI is even encouraging steelmakers to build plants elsewhere.

As Japan moves toward the close of the century, it has clearly undertaken an arduous and ambitious program. It will not be easy to wrest technological leadership away from the United States, and success will require a different set of skills than those that have made Japan the great nation it is today. At the same time, there are reasons to believe that Japan will soon attain equality, if not superiority, relative to America. MITI, at least, is confident. It predicts that Japan will continue to grow twice as fast in the 1980s as other leading developed countries.

As the *Economist* recently noted: "Many forecasters in Japan think its economy will grow at this year's rate of 4.5 percent [adjusted for inflation] until the 1990s. By then, Japan's gross national product . . . may not be far short of that of the United States, which would give the 115 million Japanese nearly twice the 225 million Americans' income per head."

19 The European Challenge

The idea of a unified Europe was reborn in 1946 with Winston Churchill's famous speech calling for a "United States of Europe." It was not until eleven years later, however, that steps were taken to bring this vision into fulfillment. In March of 1957, representatives from Belgium, France, Italy, The Netherlands, Luxembourg, and West Germany signed the Treaty of Rome, thereby creating the European Economic Community (EEC). In 1973, Ireland, Denmark, and the United Kingdom joined the original six, and Greece followed in 1981. Together, these ten countries comprise the greatest industrial force in the world. In 1980 the combined gross national product of the EEC, or Common Market, was larger than that of the United States.

The creation of this enormous free-trade zone has enabled European corporations to compete on more equal terms with American industrial giants. Between 1965 and 1980, the number of European companies ranking in the world's largest 500 corporations increased 25 percent. The number of European firms with sales over $1 billion jumped eightfold. During this same period, economic growth in Belgium, France, Italy, The Netherlands, and West Germany outpaced our own. The EEC's share of world GNP and world exports increased slightly, while our share declined in both categories.

● ● ●

ECONOMIC GROWTH: 1965–1980

	Annual GNP* Growth	*Annual Export Growth*
EEC Total	3.4%	15.7%
Belgium	3.6	15.6
France	4.2	16.5
Germany	3.3	16.3
Italy	3.7	16.6
Netherlands	3.7	16.6
United States	2.9	13.7

EEC countries hope to maintain this strong growth rate in the 1980s. To help them do so, the European Monetary System (EMS) was founded in 1979. Exchange rates among Western European nations fluctuated frequently and unexpectedly during the 1970s, and this uncertainty tended to depress intercountry trade. Corporations were never sure what the currency they were to be paid in would be worth by the time they received payment.

To solve such problems, member countries, with the exception of the United Kingdom, agreed to limit exchange rate fluctuations against other EEC currencies. In order to facilitate this, gold and member currencies were stockpiled. Whenever exchange rates change by more than 2 percentage points the EMS intervenes to stabilize the market.† By stabilizing exchange rates, the EMS should encourage increased trade and investment between member countries, at the expense of the U.S. and other nonparticipating nations.

EEC countries are also working together to move the European economy out of basic industries. A joint

---

*Real GNP, adjusted for inflation.

†Italy's currency is allowed to fluctuate by 6 percent before the EMS intervenes.

research program has been established to pursue developments in science and technology. In 1980 the EEC's research budget was approximately $400 million. Nearly 70 percent of these funds were devoted to energy research, including a major fusion-development program. Another $32 million was budgeted for a five-year research program in biogenetics. Other research money was provided for work in the area of computers and semiconductors.

These programs merely supplement the efforts of the individual member nations. West Germany, for example, whose economic growth spearheaded the European resurgence, depends on the Bundesministerium für Forschung und Technologie (BMFT) to provide direct financial support for industrial research and development in high-technology areas. With an annual budget of close to $3 billion, the agency funds almost 20 percent of all industry-related R&D expenditures. Industries that have already received considerable financial support from BMFT include aerospace, computers, nuclear energy, machine tools, semiconductors, and telecommunications.

France, whose emergence as a world industrial power has gone almost unnoticed beside the attention focused on Japan and Germany, in 1979 created the Committee for Strategic Industrial Development (CODIS) to select high-growth, high-technology industries for government support. The decision-making body of CODIS is chaired by the prime minister and includes the ministers of budget, finance, foreign trade, and industry. The committee has already conducted an exhaustive analysis of some six hundred industrial sectors and ranked each one on the basis of thirty-three criteria, including future growth, world competition, current French market share, and sources of competitive advantage. Based on this work, CODIS announced in 1980 that seven growth industries would be especially critical for France's future development: the automated office, biotechnology, consumer electronics, energy conservation equipment, robotics, new developments in textiles, and undersea exploration equipment.

The French government will promote CODIS-selected industries through the use of export credits as well as through direct grants. Credits are low-interest loans made to foreign companies or governments to encourage them to buy French goods and services. The French are especially aggressive in their use of these subsidies: 20 percent of all French exports are supported this way versus about 10 percent in most other industrialized countries. The government-owned export bank, Banque Francaise du Commerce Extérieur, maintains an outstanding loan portfolio of more than $50 billion, double the portfolio of our own Export-Import Bank. In some instances, loans are offered for only one-half the going market rate. French firms have won many foreign contracts on the strength of their financing packages alone. Through a variety of such programs, major European nations, working both individually and together, hope to make themselves first-rate powers in high technology, a strategy that will directly challenge American industrial strength in the 1980s and 1990s.

20 NICs

The 1970s witnessed the emergence of a new economic force in the world economy—the so-called newly industrialized countries (NICs). Among the most prominent are Brazil, Mexico, Hong Kong, Singapore, South Korea, and Taiwan. During the last decade these countries emerged as a significant factor in such basic industries as chemicals, construction, consumer electronics, machinery, steel, leather goods, shipbuilding, and textiles..In these and other industries, they are taking market share from the United States, Japan, and Western Europe.

The NICs' share of world industrial production has been increasing rapidly. Between the middle of the 1960s and the end of the 1970s, Mexico's share of world industrial production increased nearly 50 percent; Brazil's approximately 85 percent; Singapore's 100 percent; Hong Kong's 300 percent; Taiwan's 400 percent; and South Korea's 600 percent. In total, the NICs now account for 10 percent of the world's industrial production. During the 1970s, Brazil's gross national product grew at an annual rate of 11 percent a year after adjusting for inflation; South Korea's and Hong Kong's 10 percent; Singapore's 9 percent; and Mexico's 5 percent. This compared to an average growth rate of just over 3 percent in the United States.

Much of the success of the NICs has come about through development strategies that stress the export of manufactured goods. Products made in South Korea, Taiwan, Hong Kong, and Brazil fill department stores in New York, London, Paris, and Rome. Between 1963 and

1976, Singapore's share of world manufactured exports increased by 40 percent; Hong Kong's by 50 percent; Mexico's by 300 percent; Brazil's and Taiwan's by 800 percent; and South Korea's by 2400 percent.

A powerful new group of Third World multinational corporations has risen along with the NICs. Between 1970 and 1980, the number of corporations based in the developing world that rank among the world's 500 largest industrial corporations nearly tripled. In the forefront are the big state-owned energy firms such as Petróleas de Venezuela with 1980 sales of $18.8 billion; Petrobrás (Brazil) with sales of $14.8 billion; and PEMEX (Mexico), with sales of $14.8 billion. All three of these companies rank among the top fifty corporations in the world. Some of the leading manufacturing giants in the Third World include:

Company	*Country*	*Business*	*1980 Sales (in billions)*
Hyundai Group	South Korea	Shipbuilding	$5.5
Samsung Group	South Korea	Appliances, textiles	$3.8
Zambia Industrial & Mining	Zambia	Copper, food products	$2.7
Koç Holding	Turkey	Motor vehicles, electronics	$2.2
Formosa Plastics Group	Taiwan	Chemicals	$1.6
Valores Industriales	Mexico	Food products	$1.2
Siderúrgica Nacional	Brazil	Steel	$1.1

The emergence of strong competition from the NICs affects the American economy in several ways. First, NIC imports are flooding our home market. During the 1960s and 1970s, imports from NICs increased more than four times, and by the late 1970s, we were importing more than $10 billion in manufactured goods alone.

While we rapidly increase our NIC imports, we are not doing so well with exports. NICs have a great appetite for capital goods (machine tools, construction equipment, etc.) and high-technology products needed for their industrialization programs. For the most part, they have to buy these products abroad. As a result of such purchases, the NICs ran a cumulative trade deficit of approximately $20 billion a year with the industrialized world by the end of the 1970s. American manufacturers have not, however, participated in this bonanza. Our trade deficit with the NICs in manufactured goods has been about $3 billion.

The second major consequence of the rapid rise of NICs has been that we are losing overseas markets. This is true in both the developed and the developing world. The NICs' market share of exports of manufactured goods to industrialized countries increased by 10 percent between 1963 and 1977; during this time, the American share decreased by nearly the same amount. The trend is even more pronounced in less developed countries where the NICs' share of total manufactured exports increased by almost 75 percent.

A third consequence of NIC expansion is harder to document. There is, however, some evidence that overseas investment opportunities for American companies are being adversely affected. The Hong Kong *Standard* suggested as much in 1977: "In many cases, developing countries appear to prefer investment from other like countries to investment from a major power. For one thing such investment is less threatening. In wooing Hong Kong investors, Sri Lanka's trade minister made it clear that investors from smaller countries would receive a warmer welcome than those from the developed nations: 'We favor investors from small places like Hong Kong because nobody can talk about a sell-out to imperialism in the case of a country that is as small or smaller than we are.' " While this attitude may or may not be widespread, it is one of several factors constraining American sales abroad.

To add to our competitive troubles, a new crowd of NICs are on the way. Countries such as Chile, Kenya, Malaysia, Indonesia, and the Philippines could be the Hong Kongs and Taiwans of the future.

Malaysia is a good example of a prospective NIC. According to a study by Chase Econometrics, Malaysia will emerge as a new Southeast Asian superstar in the 1980s. The country's gross national product is expected to grow at an average rate of 8.8 percent a year adjusted for inflation during the decade and exports at 11.0 percent a year. Growth should be especially strong in steel and petrochemicals, areas where the United States is already under heavy attack.

There are three basic reasons for the emergence of NICs as a strong competitive force in the global economy. The first is cheap labor. It should come as no surprise that the developing countries are beginning to dominate labor-intensive industries such as textiles, leather goods, and consumer electronics. It is in these industries that the NICs can best exploit their labor-cost advantage.

The combined population of the developing world is already 70 percent of the world total. By the end of this century, it will rise to 80 percent, and by the middle of the next century to as much as 90 percent. With all these people looking for scarce jobs in the industrial sector, there will be a supply of very low cost labor for many years to come. Even in today's NICs, wages are sometimes below $1 an hour. This puts the industrialized world at a severe disadvantage in labor-intensive industries that are difficult or impossible to automate.

A second reason for the rise of the NICs is that industrial technologies have been diffused throughout the world at an increasingly rapid rate by multinational corporations, consulting firms, and construction firms offering complete turnkey facilities. As a result of this trend, NICs with skilled labor forces have been able to establish themselves in such industries as consumer electronics and steel, as well as more basic ones such as shoes and textiles. Over the past quarter century, twenty-five nations began to manufacture steel for the first time. The record in automobiles is even more astonishing. In the mid-1960s, fifty-five nations were assembling automobiles. By the end of the 1970s this number had increased to eighty-six and was still rising.

The third factor that has led to the rapid development of the NICs is money, especially OPEC money. As oil prices skyrocketed in the 1970s, OPEC nations found themselves with multibillion-dollar trade surpluses. These funds were often deposited in major international banks in the United States and Europe. At the same time, the growth rate of the developed world slowed in order to adjust to higher oil prices. Demand for industrial loans slowed as well.

Faced with growing deposits and falling loan demand in their traditional markets, the banks began to lend large sums to developing countries. These countries were eager to borrow in order to spur their industrialization efforts. Between 1970 and 1980, medium- and long-term loans outstanding to Third World countries rose from $60 million to $450 billion. The heaviest borrowers were Brazil, Mexico, and South Korea.

Thus armed with low-cost labor, modern technology, and extensive financing, the NICs have become formidable competitors in a wide array of industrial markets. They should become even stronger in future years as they

shift further from light manufacturing into heavy manufacturing and higher technologies. Development expert
Juergen Donges, of West Germany's Kiel Institute of
World Economics, believes that by the end of this century Third World countries will dominate such industries
as steel, automobiles, shipping, consumer electronics,
metal fabricating, and petrochemicals.

21 The China Factor

China is the "wild card" of the new global economy, and its emergence from past isolation is sure to have a profound impact on the world balance of economic power. The timing and nature of this impact, however, is still obscure.

In 1978, China's new leaders announced a $350 billion industrialization program involving 120 large-scale projects. Included in this total were thirty power stations, ten steel plants, nine nonferrous metal complexes, eight coal mines, six railways, and five new harbors. All of these were to be built by 1985.

By 1981, however, it had become clear that they had tried to do too much too soon. A combination of insufficient foreign reserves, bad planning, a lack of the necessary infrastructure to support a modernization program of such scale, and rising inflation (estimated at between 10 and 15 percent in 1980) forced a curtailment of the industrial drive. Capital spending was reduced by 40 percent in 1980 alone. Many of the 120 super projects were scrapped altogether, while others were substantially cut back.

Despite this momentary retreat from industrialization, China continues to make tremendous strides in labor-intensive industries. Output in light manufacturing industries such as bicycles, radios, and textiles increased 20 percent in 1980 alone. If growth continues at this pace, China will be able to build the necessary market share to become a feared competitor in the international economy.

China may also become a major exporter of energy. Potential petroleum reserves have been estimated at 50 to 80 billion barrels (compared to Saudi Arabia's reserves of 163 billion and U.S. reserves of 27 billion). Oil production has increased by 20 percent a year for more than a decade and already ranks tenth in the world. By developing both its oil and extensive coal reserves, China should be able to earn sufficient hard currency to spur its industrialization efforts.

Despite these strengths, however, it will be many years before China is able to challenge the U.S. in heavy manufacturing or high-technology industries. From the short-term point of view, the major question about China is whether it will decide to open its market to the outside world. Countries and corporations that are able to penetrate China's market successfully will have a tremendous new opportunity to build world market share.

American exports to China between 1978 and 1980 totaled $6.3 billion, with grain accounting for a majority of our sales. Our exports trailed both Japan and Western Europe. For the moment, Japan seems to have the inside track on the Chinese market. The two nations signed an eight-year, $20 billion trade agreement in 1978, which spurred Japanese exports of $11.4 billion in the following two years. Western Europe, led by West Germany, exported $7.9 billion worth of goods to the People's Republic during the same period.

The American government is doing very little to assist our manufacturers in their efforts to capture the China trade. In 1980, as a result of strong pressure from the textile lobby, we imposed import quotas on Chinese textiles. This action was taken even though China is only the fifth-largest textile exporter to the U.S. These tariffs outraged the Chinese, whose trade balance with the U.S. in 1980 was a negative $2.5 billion. Commenting on the quotas, Huang Jianmo, second secretary at the Chinese embassy in Washington, D.C., noted: "We don't want to make a big problem, but this will affect our relations. . . . The trade balance is five to one in your favor."

While the textile quotas have put a damper on increased American trade with China, President Reagan's promise to improve relations with Taiwan could be far more damaging. China has made it clear that it will not give ground on the Taiwan issue. In 1981 Chinese officials broke off negotiations with Royal Dutch Shell over possible oil exploration rights after the Dutch government agreed to sell submarines to the Taiwanese. If the U.S. hopes to gain access to the Chinese market, the president will have to soften his pro-Taiwan stance. The opportunity to build world market share in China is a unique opportunity that should not be allowed to slip away.

22 The "Sick Man" of the East

The most interesting fact about the Soviet Union today is that it has decided against full-fledged membership in the world economy. This decision on the part of the Kremlin has already proven fateful.

It could be argued that the Soviet leadership never really had a choice. Russian leaders from the earliest days of the czars have regarded the outside world with latent or overt hostility and have feared the infiltration of Western ideas accompanying trade and technology. Yet even with this long tradition of quasi-isolation, Soviet leaders could have moved more forcefully to integrate their country into the world economy. By failing to do so, they have jeopardized the sizable economic gains achieved during the post-Stalin era.

By 1980, the consequences of continuing Soviet isolation were already apparent. Economic growth had slowed to 1.5 percent a year, only one-quarter the rate of the 1950s. Gross national product per person was still less than half that of the United States and the gap was not closing. Moreover, the economy was gripped by a series of long-term problems—all of which were likely to grow worse without major infusions of outside technology.

Probably the most serious of these problems was stagnant labor productivity. Productivity increased at the rate of 3.5 percent a year during the 1960s. In the 1970s, however, this fell to 1.5 percent. In 1979 and 1980, productivity growth was zero.

In the past, the Soviets tried to compensate for poor productivity by increasing the number of workers, but this strategy is no longer viable. Population growth in the U.S.S.R. has virtually come to a standstill. Indeed, the Soviet Union is the only industrialized country in the world in which average life expectancy is falling and infant mortality is increasing.

The population will expand somewhat in the next two decades, but growth will be concentrated in the outlying Muslim and Turkic regions of the empire, and these areas have never participated fully in the Soviet economy. As a result, Soviet leaders face a serious demographic challenge. In their industrial heartland, many more skilled workers will reach retirement age than will enter the labor force. To avoid serious labor shortages, Asiatic Russians will have to be brought into the system.

Even without the skilled labor shortages expected in the future, industry is already in a state of decline. Production of both steel and coal, traditionally strong in the Soviet economy, fell in 1979 and again in 1980. Investment in new plant and equipment is increasing more slowly than ever before. Capital spending increased by only 2.0 percent in 1979 and by 1.7 percent in 1980.

Agriculture also remains a serious problem. Bad weather is a perennial threat in much of Russia. Because of weather and other factors, agricultural output actually declined in both 1979 and 1980. As a result, the Soviets have had to import substantial amounts of grain from the West—30 million metric tons in 1980 alone.

The only bright spot for the Soviets in recent years has been oil. Russia is the largest producer of oil in the world. In 1980, an average of 12 million barrels of crude were pumped per day versus 9 million in Saudi Arabia. By selling their production in the world market, the Russians have been able to earn vital hard currency. In 1979, Soviet oil exports earned $9.5 billion, money that was used to buy capital equipment and technology from the West.

By producing so much oil, however, the U.S.S.R. is starting to drain its reserves. At present, these are only one-half the size of Saudi Arabia's. In the future, the Soviets will be forced to reduce exports.

The CIA has predicted that Russia will actually become a net importer of oil by 1985. While the CIA forecast has been disputed by other authorities, it is clear that oil will not produce hard currency revenues indefinitely. Proposed sales of natural gas to Western Europe could help offset oil revenue losses to a degree, but cannot completely do so.

The Russians' economic woes are compounded by those of their Eastern European satellites, as well as by those of satellites in other parts of the world. The Soviet Union continues to prop up Cuba's ailing economy by selling oil to Cuba at $13 a barrel and by purchasing large amounts of sugar at favorable prices. Economic aid to Vietnam in the form of grain, oil, and technology runs more than $1 billion a year. Subsidies of this kind are estimated to cost the Soviets more than $20 billion annually. Added to this are special assistance for Poland and Soviet military ventures in Afghanistan and elsewhere that place further strain on an already depressed economy.

The Russians could have avoided many of these problems by choosing to moderate their military and political goals in favor of active participation in the global marketplace. For competing there would have forced Soviet industries to be more efficient. It would also have allowed the Soviets to concentrate their economic resources in areas where they possess a competitive advantage. Most importantly, participating in the global economy would have offered them access to the latest high technologies. Soviet labor shortages and productivity shortfalls in particular could be addressed with industrial robots and CAD/CAM. As it is, Russia already trails the West in these important areas by five to ten years, and without these key technologies, its industry is virtually doomed to fall even further behind.

Part Five

America's Export Giants

23 The American Breadbasket

Agriculture is America's biggest and most successful international business. Our farmers produce 80 percent of the world's corn exports, 70 percent of soybean exports, and 50 percent of wheat exports. We are also the world's leading exporter of a variety of other agricultural crops and products including cotton, rice, lettuce, tobacco, and almonds.

In 1980, agricultural exports reached $41.3 billion. This was the tenth consecutive year in which farm exports established a new high. As a result, our positive trade balance in agricultural products exceeded $23 billion and provided the largest single check on our mounting trade deficit. Over the last decade, we exported agricultural goods worth $228 billion and produced a cumulative surplus of $111 billion. According to a Department of Agriculture study, more than one million full-time jobs are directly related to agricultural exports.

For a variety of reasons relating to national security as well as export earnings, it is imperative that America maintain a strong agricultural base. In the near future, we should have little trouble. Although the growth rate of our agricultural exports may slow, we should continue to dominate world agricultural markets at least through this decade.

In the long run, however, there is cause for concern. Brazil is mounting an aggressive agricultural export campaign and has already taken control of several markets formerly dominated by the United States. Meanwhile, our agricultural productivity has begun to

stagnate after decades of steady progress and our crop-
lands—perhaps the country's most valuable natural
resource—are slowly being eroded away. If all these factors work against us, our future in agriculture may not
turn out to be as bright as many people believe.

The most immediate threat to our agricultural
supremacy lies in Brazil. With 3.3 million square miles
of land, Brazil is larger than the United States excluding
Alaska, and has an abundant supply of fertile cropland.
With only 25 percent of the country's potential farmland
under cultivation, Brazil has already become the world's
second-largest exporter of agricultural commodities. In
1980 its agricultural exports totaled $20.1 billion, pri-
marily in coffee, sugar, cocoa, soybeans, oranges, beef,
and chicken.

After twenty years of investment in its infrastructure
(roads, waterways, railroads) and technology (fertilizer,
machinery, education), Brazil is now ready to challenge
American world leadership in several markets, the most
important of which is soybeans—our second-biggest cash
crop after corn. In 1980, the total value of the American
soybean crop exceeded $13.8 billion. Soybeans ac-
counted for approximately one-third of our total agricultural exports.

Soybeans are native to Southeast Asia, but grow
exceedingly well in Midwest America—Iowa, Illinois,
Indiana, Minnesota, and Ohio. Soybeans can be used as
either high-protein meal for animal feedstocks or in
human foods such as tofu. They are also ground into oil
for use in salad dressings, margarines, cooking oils, and
shortenings. Industrial uses of soybeans include paint,
soap, cement, and pesticides.

Although American farmers still supply a majority of
the world's soybeans, our share of world exports has
steadily declined from 97 percent in the late 1960s to less
than 70 percent by the end of the 1970s. During the same
period, Brazil's market share has risen to 15 percent

from less than one percent. By making production and export of soybeans a cornerstone of its agricultural policy, the Brazilian government has been able to increase production 2000 percent during the past twenty years. As a result, soybeans have become one of Brazil's most important sources of hard currency. Spurred by further subsidies, Brazilian output should continue its rapid expansion in future years.

But soybeans are not the only area that Brazil has targeted for a major export effort. Brazil has already surpassed us as the world's leading exporter of frozen concentrated orange juice. Much of the Brazilian product is sold here despite a tariff equal to one-third of selling price. Brazilian farmers also lead in the export of chickens.

Will American farmers be able to maintain their competitiveness in the face of challenges from Brazil and other nations? The answer ultimately depends on our ability to remain the low-cost producer of agricultural products. Unfortunately, our recent productivity gains in the agricultural sector have not been very encouraging. Between 1950 and 1970, productivity increased at a rate of 1.7 percent a year, but in the 1970s it fell to 1.5 percent. This compares to a worldwide average of 2.0 percent. If this trend continues, as some analysts predict, it could seriously jeopardize our long-term competitive position. An unpublished study by an economist at the Department of Agriculture indicates that Australia has already supplanted the U.S. as the world's lowest-cost producer of wheat. It could be only the beginning.

One reason for the recent productivity slide is that investment in agricultural research and development has tapered off. Agricultural research in the 1970s, measured as a percentage of industry sales, was less than in the 1950s and 1960s. In addition, an increasing amount of agriculture research budgets is being used to meet federal regulations. According to a report by the Agriculture Council of America, 35 to 40 percent of R&D expenditures in the field of agricultural chemicals are devoted to compliance with regulatory standards on toxicology and other environmental concerns. While such funds are well spent if they protect human health, they cannot take the place of conventional R&D aimed at improving crop productivity. With genetic manipulation and other new techniques on the horizon, the United States should be doubling or even tripling its agricultural research budget.

A problem potentially even greater than inadequate research is the way we abuse our farmland resources. According to a 1981 Department of Agriculture study, we have 413 million acres of cropland and 127 million acres of potential cropland. But we are losing 3 million acres per year to such nonagricultural uses as shopping centers, residential developments, highways, and manmade lakes. As our own population increases, we will need more acreage just to feed ourselves. At some point, our capacity for export may be curtailed.

As we continue to consume valuable farmland, we are also failing to conserve water and soil resources. One-quarter of the water we use comes from vast underground deposits called aquifers. Our annual reliance on these deposits now exceeds 25 trillion gallons a year. Farmlands in Nebraska, Kansas, Colorado, New Mexico, Oklahoma, and Texas are especially dependent on a single aquifer—virtually an underground sea—called the Ogallala.

The problem with aquifers is that they are only partly renewable resources. At the present time, we are using 21 billion gallons of water a day over and above what can be returned by rainfall. As a result, scientists estimate that critical aquifers such as the Ogallala could dry up within forty years. In California's lush San Joaquin Valley, parts of the land where water has been pumped out of the ground in large quantities have already subsided thirty feet, thereby permanently damaging the aquifer. Unless we change our ways, such misuse of our water resources could have grave consequences for our future as an agricultural power.

Abuse of our soil resources is of even more immediate concern. Fertile topsoil, the key to high-yielding crops, is not an unlimited natural resource. Throughout most of America, it varies in depth from a couple of inches to a couple of feet. Each year a certain amount of this soil is lost through wind erosion or drained into rivers. Scientists estimate that an acre of land can lose up to five tons of soil a year without serious damage, since an equivalent amount of soil can be created each year through natural processes. If losses exceed this amount, however, fertility is reduced. Studies indicate that the United States is currently losing twice as much topsoil per year as can be replaced by nature. The Department of Agriculture reports that we are losing 5 billion tons of topsoil every year and that current erosion rates in the Midwest could eventually reduce soybean and corn yields by as much as 30 percent.

In 1979, Assistant Secretary of Agriculture Rupert Cutler told Congress that "soil erosion is now worse than in the Dust Bowl days." In the Dust Bowl days of the 1930s, soil erosion was so bad that tough conservation laws were passed. Despite these laws, a 1981 Council on Environmental Quality study warned that 225 million acres of American farmland were experiencing "severe desertification." John Timmons, a professor at Iowa State, has warned: "In the years ahead, soil erosion and water-quality problems appear likely to replace petroleum as the nation's most critical natural resource problem."

24 Chemical Warfare

> The U.S. chemical industry will face new challenges as a result of increased foreign competition during the 1980s. . . . . European and Japanese firms will extend their U.S. ventures. And Third World chemical producers will enter the markets.
> —*Chemical Week*, May 21, 1980

Full-scale chemical warfare may soon break out in the United States. This battle will not be fought with nerve gas or napalm, but rather with ethylene, ammonia, sulfur, petrochemicals, aspirin, super glue, and even Alka-Seltzer. The battle will be for control of our $170 billion chemical industry, which employs nearly one million people. The American chemical market accounts for one-third of world chemical sales, and everyone wants a piece of it. Preparing to lead the attack are West Germany, France, Japan, and a host of developing countries.

American firms currently control the major part of their home market. With superior technology, high productivity, and cheaper access to raw materials, firms such as DuPont, Dow Chemical, Union Carbide, Monsanto, and Celanese have established America as the world leader in chemicals. Our strength is such that in 1980 we enjoyed a $14 billion positive balance of trade in this one industry. Whether we will be able to maintain a positive balance of this magnitude in future years is very much in doubt.

Leading the attack on our home market is West Germany. Three German corporations, Hoechst, Bayer, and BASF, have emerged as the world's largest chemical companies. Their respective 1980 sales of $16.4 billion, $15.9 billion, and $15.3 billion place them well ahead of DuPont's $13.6 billion. As recently as 1969, DuPont was the world leader. Having established their dominance in the European market, the three German firms have now turned their attention to the United States. Present plans call for doubling or even tripling their $5 billion in American sales by the end of the 1980s.

As Kurt Lanz, deputy chairman of Hoechst, has stated, "No market in the world is more important to Hoechst today than the U.S. Our hope is to have American Hoechst rank as a major chemicals and pharmaceutical company in its own right." In pursuit of this objective, Hoechst is spending $180 million to build a petrochemical plant in Bayport, Texas. The company is also increasing its pharmaceutical sales force in the United States by 50 percent in an effort to double sales by 1985.

Bayer and BASF are following a somewhat different strategy. They are trying to buy their way into the market by purchasing established U.S. companies. Between them, they have bought seven American firms including Elkhart, Inc., the maker of Alka-Seltzer.

Where the Germans have gained a beachhead, the French will soon follow. After increasing their chemical exports by 50 percent between 1975 and 1980, the French are now the world's third-largest exporter of chemicals after Germany and the United States. French companies hope to continue this expansion by making deeper inroads into the American market. As *Chemical Week*, an industry publication of McGraw-Hill, noted about French chemical companies: "Getting into the U.S. . . . is in everyone's plans these days."

The Japanese also have designs on the American market. Japanese chemical companies have opened offices in the United States for marketing and research purposes and expect to begin manufacturing here as well. On a small scale, the Japanese invasion has already begun—in 1980 two Japanese chemical companies announced plans to build manufacturing facilities in California for the production of super glue.

As in other industries, Japanese chemical manufacturers are actively supported by government agencies. To promote technology and economies of scale, the Ministry of International Trade and Industry is encouraging corporate consolidations and joint research projects funded with government money. One such program has brought twenty-three major chemical and oil companies together at a cost of $150 million to pursue advances in petrochemicals (chemicals derived from oil and gas).

Japan is an especially dangerous foe in the pharmaceutical market. Its pharmaceutical firms have increased their expenditures on research and development from one percent of sales in 1965 to 7.5 percent in 1980. This investment is paying off, for their firms have emerged as world leaders in the development of anticancer drugs. Two of the most effective antibiotics recently released in the U.S. market, Moxalactam and Cefizox, were developed by Japanese companies. The Japanese are also marketing an artificial substitute for blood—a major medical breakthrough that could revolutionize transfusions. The product was originally developed by an American, but a Japanese company first recognized the potential and secured rights.

As a result of such advances, Japanese revenues from licensing drugs to foreign manufacturers increased nearly four times during the 1970s. World sales of the ten largest Japanese drug companies increased at an average rate of 30 to 60 percent between 1975 and 1978. By contrast, the growth rate of the ten largest American companies was only 8 to 13 percent a year. Partly because of

Japanese success, nine of the ten largest American pharmaceutical firms lost world market share between 1975 and 1980.

Yet perhaps the biggest challenge to our chemical industry will come in the petrochemical market, which is worth more than $70 billion a year in the U.S. alone. It is a market that OPEC nations eventually hope to dominate. Saudi Arabia is currently spending $35 billion to build seven giant petrochemical complexes and the necessary infrastructure to support the industry. All seven of the Saudi plants should be in operation by 1985. Kuwait, Turkey, Libya, Oman, Qatar, and The United Arab Emirates are also building such plants. Southeast Asian countries with large supplies of natural gas are only a step behind. Indonesia, Malaysia, the Philippines, Singapore, and Taiwan plan to spend more than $17 billion to establish petrochemical industries. OECD's "Facing the Future" report predicts that the developing world will eventually acquire "significant" market share in petrochemicals.

The proliferation of potential petrochemical competitors comes at a time when American companies are suffering the impact of energy price decontrol in the United States. For most of the period after 1973, American producers were able to buy domestic oil and gas at prices far below the world market. By the end of 1981, however, American oil prices had risen to world levels. Gas prices are expected to be totally deregulated by 1985, if not sooner. This means that the American industry has lost its cost advantage at the same time that new and potentially much lower cost competitors are appearing on the horizon.

Will the American chemical industry survive this tightening vise of competition? Unfortunately, the signs of retreat are all too evident:

• Although we still enjoy a healthy trade balance,

imports increased faster than exports throughout the 1970s.

• Spending on research and development, the heart of the industry, has fallen. Chemical producers spent nearly 4 percent of sales on R&D in the early 1960s, but only slightly more than 2 percent in 1980. By comparison, the big three West German firms spent over 4 percent of their sales on R&D.

• Because of their failure to maintain R&D expenditures, American chemical companies are beginning to lose their technological edge. Pharmaceuticals provide only one example. Hoechst has more new drugs ready to enter the U.S. market than does any American firm. The German company has five times the number of drugs awaiting approval from the U.S. Federal Drug Administration than Merck, the largest prescription drug manufacturer in America.

• Productivity is slowing. Physical output per man hour in the American chemical industry increased by 8.4 percent a year between 1960 and 1965, slowed to 7.1 percent a year between 1970 and 1976, and fell to 6.1 percent a year between 1977 and 1980.

• Investment in new plant and equipment is declining. The *Kline Guide to the Chemical Industry*, an authoritative source, estimates that capital investment will fall to 7.0 percent of sales by 1985 from a high of 9.5 in 1966.

• The industry is stuck in a regulatory maze. Chemicals is one of the most heavily regulated industries in the United States. Other governments are less concerned about air and water pollution, solid waste disposal, and worker safety. While American companies must be kept to a high standard in these areas, current regulations are often confusing, contradictory, and needlessly expensive. Matters are further complicated by the multiplicity of political jurisdictions.

Unless these trends are reversed, the chemical industry

may soon find itself in serious trouble. The time to take countermeasures is now. Much of the competition that is expected in the 1980s is still gathering strength. If we wait much longer before taking corrective action, it could be too late.

25 Airbus Takes Off

Since the days of the Wright Brothers, American companies have dominated the world market for commercial and private airplanes, military aircraft, helicopters, and aircraft engines. In 1980, sales of these products exceeded $50 billion and provided over one million jobs. A trade surplus of $13 billion placed aerospace just behind agriculture and chemicals as our third-most successful export industry. Among the twenty largest American exporting companies, eight are in some way involved in aerospace.

The major part of aerospace export earnings have come from commercial jet aircraft sales. Three multibillion-dollar American firms, Boeing, McDonnell Douglas, and Lockheed, have traditionally ruled this marketplace. As recently as the mid-1970s, these companies accounted for approximately 95 percent of all orders placed for wide-bodied commercial jets in the Western World. Of the three firms, Seattle-based Boeing is the largest and most dominant. With its family of commercial aircraft, ranging from the 100-seat 737 to the 452-seat jumbo 747, Boeing has sold 60 percent of all passenger jets built in the Western World.

Today, however, the American position in the commercial jet market is being strongly challenged by a consortium of English, French, Spanish, and West German firms known as Airbus Industries. By combining their engineering, manufacturing, and financial resources, these European firms were able to design a new medium-range, wide-bodied, 260-passenger jet that no existing American product design could match.

The Airbus plane, the A-300, was developed in 1973 and proved to be perfectly suited for medium-range flights in and around Europe. Its wide body not only offered passengers additional comfort, but more importantly, used one-third less fuel per passenger. After a slow beginning, in which only fifty orders were received in the consortium's first five years, Airbus sales have grown rapidly. Since 1978, more than 200 orders have been placed for the A-300. Based on the success of the A-300, the consortium decided to build a smaller Airbus, the A-310, with room for 210 passengers. Nearly eighty of these airplanes have already been ordered. In total, orders and options for both Airbus models now exceed $15 billion.

Following Airbus' success, Boeing developed its own medium-range, wide-bodied jet, the 767, which holds 210 people. The 767 competes directly against the two Airbus models. At the same time, Boeing also introduced a new twin-engine plane, the 757, which will seat 178 passengers. The 767 is scheduled to begin regular commercial service in 1982 and the 757 in 1983.

Both Boeing planes have been well received by American airline companies. More than 160 firm orders have been placed for the 767 and more than 100 for the 757, most of them from Boeing's traditional big customers: American, Delta, TWA, and United. Delta Airlines alone ordered sixty of the 757s at a cost of $3 billion— the largest single purchase in aviation history.

But the 757 and 767 have not been so successful in Europe. In fact, Boeing has received only one order for the 757 from a major European carrier, British Airways. Even this sale did not come easily. British Airways is a state-owned company and its executives were heavily criticized for not choosing a British-subsidized Airbus plane. In order to placate its critics, BA publicly announced that Airbus would "best meet its needs" for a medium-range, wide-bodied plane in the future.

The other major European Airline companies, Air France, Germany's Lufthansa, Swiss Air, the Dutch KLM, and British Caledonia have all opted for Airbus planes over the new Boeing models. The consortium has also been successful in the Third World, receiving orders from Cruzeiro Brazilian Airlines, Varig Brazilian Airlines, Korean Airlines, Singapore Airlines, Thai International, Malaysian Airlines, and Pakistan International.

Airbus has even won a major contract in the United States. In 1978, Eastern Airlines ordered twenty-three Airbus planes at a cost of $778 million. This marked the first time in fifteen years that an American firm had gone outside the United States to order a commercial jet. In announcing the decision to buy its planes from the European consortium, Eastern President Frank Borman, the former astronaut, said: "What concerns me most is the U.S. technology that was once the best in the world has not kept pace. The A-300 is here when we need it."

Despite Borman's statement, a key factor in Eastern's choice of Airbus was the attractive financial package offered. Eastern received a government-backed low-interest loan with exceptionally easy repayment provisions for half of the total sales price. Airbus has offered similar financial packages to other airline companies in order to win sales. Testifying before Congress on such government-subsidized loans, Boeing's treasurer said: "We can compete with Airbus and the other European manufacturers on cost and technical merits, but we cannot compete with the national treasuries of France and Germany and other European countries."

To rectify this situation, the American government in 1981 reached an agreement with the governments of Britain, France, and West Germany to charge common interest rates on airplane sales. While this removed one government subsidy, it did not necessarily solve the problem. European manufacturers can still use government backing to cut prices instead of interest rates.

The major losers since Airbus' emergence have been McDonnell Douglas and Lockheed. In 1976 Boeing received 34 percent of all orders for wide-bodied jet airplanes, Lockheed 34 percent, McDonnell Douglas 29 percent, and Airbus 3 percent. By 1979 Airbus had captured 38 percent of the market, leaving Boeing with 37 percent, McDonnell Douglas with only 13 percent, and Lockheed with just 12 percent. Airbus' backlog of orders now exceeds the combined backlog of McDonnell Douglas and Lockheed.

As a result of their declining market shares, both American companies have lost considerable amounts of money. Losses for Lockheed became so great that in 1981 the firm announced that it was getting out of the commercial jet business altogether. The firm said that total losses on its TriStar program amounted to $2.5 billion. McDonnell Douglas' commercial aircraft division reported losses of $55 million in 1979 and $144 million in 1980.

While Boeing remains a healthy company, its recent problems in Europe and the Third World are cause for concern. In past years, nearly 50 percent of the company's sales have been to non-U.S.-based airlines. Losing a substantial part of the rapidly growing overseas market could seriously cripple the company's ability to commit the billions of dollars needed to design new aircraft.

Airbus will make things as difficult as possible for Boeing. The consortium is expecting to triple its production schedule in 1982 and quadruple it in 1983. Current plans are to build a whole family of wide-bodied jets, ranging from 130 to 345 seats. The first new plane in this series, the A-320, has already been announced and will come in 130- and 160-passenger versions. Perhaps even more disturbing is the possibility that the Europeans may

offer Japan a share in the consortium. Japanese participation would certainly strengthen Airbus and represent a
blow to American manufacturers.

Even if the Japanese do not join Airbus, they will be
heard from on their own. Ministry of International
Trade and Industry officials have indicated that they
want Japan to become a major aerospace manufacturer
in the future. Although the Japanese currently trail both
U.S. and European manufacturers in aerospace technology, they are catching up quickly. In order to speed their
learning process, several Japanese companies have entered into agreements with Boeing to manufacture sections of the 767. Mitsubishi and Kawasaki will build
parts for the body of the plane, and Fujitsu will build a
part of the wings. Fifteen percent of the total 767 program will be built in Japan. The Japanese hope that by
working with Boeing they will be able to learn both the
engineering and manufacturing skills that will one day
allow them to become a major force in the industry. As a
result of the 767 contracts, over 100 Japanese engineers
have visited Seattle to study Boeing's techniques. Nobo-
ru Hatakeyma, director of the Ministry of Trade's aircraft division, has stated that "this program might
become the special impetus for the modernization of the
Japanese industry."

As the 1980s unfold, American aerospace manufacturers will be increasingly pressed to maintain their current
market shares. McDonnell Douglas may be driven out of
the commercial jet market. Even Boeing would have
trouble competing against a new Airbus consortium that
included the Japanese.

The stakes are high. Aging fleets, the need for more
fuel-efficient planes, and ever-increasing regulations re-
garding noise and other standards ensure that major airline companies all over the world will be making large
purchases of new commercial jets in the 1980s. Total
sales are expected to be between $100 and $150 billion.
We cannot afford to be left out of this huge market.

26 The Unfriendly Skies

The commercial jet market is not the only sector of the aerospace industry in which American firms are facing strong competition. Markets for commuter aircraft, helicopters, jet engines, and military equipment are just as fiercely contested.

Losses to date have been most severe in the area of commuter aircraft—small planes carrying from fifteen to sixty people. Foreign competitors now control 27 percent of the American market and appear certain to capture an even larger share.

The rapid decline of American commuter aircraft manufacturers can be traced to the Airline Deregulation Act of 1978. The act allows major airlines to discontinue unprofitable flight routes if they are picked up by a commuter company. The major airlines wanted to discontinue service on lightly traveled routes because rising fuel costs made their large planes increasingly uneconomical to operate with low passenger loads. Commuter airlines with smaller, more gas-efficient planes could still make a profit on such flights and were eager to claim additional routes.

Deregulation thus created a need for more commuter aircraft. At the same time, the commuter airlines wanted different—not just additional—planes. They wanted more room than the traditional fifteen seats and more fuel efficient turboprop planes that combined a jet engine with a propeller. American manufacturers, however, were overly cautious and would not develop a new generation of planes until they were sure that a market would materialize. When deregulation passed, there was only one American company, Swearingen Aviation, manufacturing a turboprop airplane with more than fifteen seats.

With American manufacturers unprepared to meet their needs, commuter airlines turned to foreign manufacturers. Foreign firms were well established in the market before deregulation, but passage of the act gave them additional momentum. Canada's de Havilland Aircraft, Brazil's Embrarer, and Ireland's Short Brothers were already manufacturing large turboprop commuter planes for their home markets and seized upon the opportunity to expand their position in the United States.

According to the Commuter Airline Association, orders for commuter aircraft between 1978 and 1980 reached $1 billion or twice the value of the entire commuter fleet before deregulation. More than 75 percent of these new orders went to foreign manufacturers. The biggest winner was de Havilland, which in only two years received seventy orders for its new fifty-seat, $5 million Dash 7 turboprop jet.

American manufacturers are only now beginning to produce the type of turboprop aircraft that is in demand. The first of these new jets, the Beech 99 and the Ahrens 404, were scheduled to be unveiled in 1981, and four other American-built planes should be on the market by 1984. But it may already be too late. Seven new foreign planes will also be introduced during the same period. Including these new models, foreign manufacturers will offer nearly twice as many large turboprop aircraft as American manufacturers.

The Federal Aviation Administration estimates that between 1980 and 2000, the market for commuter aircraft in the United States will more than double to $8 billion. Only a few years ago, most of this money would have gone to American firms, providing jobs for American workers; now most sales will probably go to foreign companies.

The blame for losing our hold on a once promising market should be placed primarily on American manufacturers. But other factors—especially the regulatory maze in which these companies operated—are also responsible. The airline industry was under control of the federal government for so long that no one could be really sure if the industry was going to be deregulated or what the results would be. Without the uncertainty and sudden change created by the regulators, American commuter manufacturers might still dominate their market.

Another important factor is that foreign manufacturers have received strong support from their respective governments. De Havilland is 100 percent government owned; Embrarer 51 percent. Government subsidies in each case reduce the risk of investing in new designs and plants. Brazil also imposes steep tariffs on imported commuter aircraft that make it virtually impossible for American firms to penetrate the Brazilian market even though the U.S. market is still wide open for Embrarer. Moreover, as with commercial jets, foreign firms have an advantage in the financial terms they can offer potential customers.

The story of commuter aircraft is being repeated, albeit more slowly, in the helicopter market. Worldwide sales in helicopters used for commercial purposes exceeded $2 billion in 1980. Textron's Bell Helicopter, United Technologies' Sikorsky Aircraft, and Summa Corporation's Hughes Helicopter, all American-based firms, have long been the world leaders in this market. But today they are being challenged by France's government-backed Aérospatiale, which has already won about 20 percent of the American market for commercial helicopters and, according to some experts, should double its current market share by 1985.

Aérospatiale's success stems directly from a ten-year, $500 million research program designed to develop a new generation of commercial helicopters. The program began in 1974 when commercial sales of helicopters were still a small segment of a market dominated by military aircraft. Aérospatiale anticipated that the 1970s would see a rapidly growing commercial market with increased use of helicopters by private business, especially oil companies and television stations. Aérospatiale was right. Today the civilian helicopter market is the fastest-growing segment of the world aerospace industry. Failing to recognize the strength of this trend, Bell, Hughes, and Sikorsky held back the investment needed to keep pace with Aérospatiale, and as a result, Aérospatiale is now the technological leader in the industry and is drawing an ever increasing share of new orders. Even the American Coast Guard has placed a $215 million order for ninety French helicopters.

Aérospatiale is taking steps to position itself for the future as well. It is exploiting what promises to be a lucrative market for helicopters in Third World countries. The company has built plants in Brazil and Indonesia and has signed a licensing agreement with China. There is also speculation that the French company might form a joint venture with Europe's three other giant helicopter manufacturers—MBB of West Germany, Agusta of Italy, and Westland of Great Britain—to develop the next generation of helicopters. If an agreement is worked out, it will spell even more trouble for American companies.

American leadership is also being challenged in a third and even more critical market—jet engines. In this case, the pride of the British government is at stake. The British initially devoted $500 million to salvage jet engine and luxury car manufacturer Rolls-Royce from bankruptcy. With this money and subsequent cash infusions ($400 million in 1980 alone), Rolls-Royce has developed a series of new jet engines. As a result, the company has emerged as a major competitor against two American firms, United Technologies' subsidiary, Pratt & Whitney, and General Electric. Analysts expect that jet engine sales will total $20 to $25 billion during the 1980s and all three companies want to supply engines for Boeing and Airbus' new airplanes.

Although Pratt & Whitney and General Electric are generally acknowledged to offer superior technology (their engines provide better gas mileage, among other factors), Rolls-Royce could still win a large share of the market. When Pan Am bought several Lockheed L-1011s in 1977, it decided to have them mounted with Rolls-Royce engines in order to benefit from British government financial aid. According to United Technologies' chairman, Harry Gray: "By choosing Rolls-Royce engines, Pan Am was able to get extremely generous loans . . . for the entire cost of the aircraft with backing from Britain's export credits guarantee department. If Pan Am had opted for our engines, such loan guarantees would not have been available and $75 million down payment would have been required. We did not lose to Rolls-Royce. Rather, we were beaten by the British government."

Rolls-Royce has enjoyed other successes including orders from British Airways (also government owned) and Eastern Airlines. The company has also contracted with leading Japanese firms to co-develop a new jet engine for smaller Airbus models that are planned for the future. If the Japanese and the British governments combine forces, even General Electric may find itself outmatched.

In the coming years, U.S. aerospace firms could also lose a significant share of the world market for military aircraft, rockets, and missiles. NATO countries have traditionally bought a substantial part of their military equipment from the United States—much of which is aerospace related—while the U.S. has bought little in return. This is not as inequitable as it might appear, since the United States bears a disproportionate share of NATO and world defense costs. Western European governments nevertheless insist that they want more of the arms trade for themselves. West Germany, which bought $4 billion worth of U.S. military equipment between 1970 and 1978, but sold no such equipment to the U.S., has been particularly adamant about this.

The immediate target of Western European aerospace firms is the market for military aircraft, worth $12 billion in sales to American firms in 1979 alone. Four aerospace companies from Britain, Holland, Italy, and West Germany have combined forces to produce the Tornado fighter-bomber, a multipurpose combat aircraft, for which the consortium has already received more than 800 orders. Moreover, West Germany plans to replace its current air defense force, which is based on McDonnell Douglas' F-4s, with an aircraft built in Europe and designed specifically for German needs.

The Europeans expect to develop their own missiles and rockets as well. In the mid-1970s, the French and Germans pooled their rocket and missile resources to form an organization called Euromissile. The British recently joined as well, adding additional political clout to the consortium. If Airbus is indicative of the political power which a European consortium can wield, American manufacturers will probably find themselves excluded from the entire Western European market.

Looking at the American aerospace industry in general, one is struck by the complexity and intensity of the competition. How well our manufacturers will stand up to this competition remains to be seen, but so far, the prognosis is not favorable. Aerospace imports to the United States increased by an alarming 73 percent in 1979 and 94 percent in 1980. The Department of Commerce expects that foreign shares of both the American and the world aerospace markets will increase in the 1980s. The story sounds all too familiar.

27 *"Encircle Caterpillar"*

Americans have always prided themselves on an ability to build things bigger and better than anyone else. Insofar as this has been true, it is because we have had the biggest and best construction machinery.

American firms have long controlled the world market for construction machinery, also referred to as earth-moving equipment. Such machinery includes bulldozers, tractors, dump trucks, steam rollers, cranes, and hydraulic excavators. Sales of this type of equipment in the United States alone exceeded $10 billion in 1980; sales outside this country represented another $10 billion. American manufacturers were able to supply nearly 50 percent of total world exports. As a result, construction machinery produced a much needed $5 billion trade surplus in 1980.

A single company, Caterpillar Tractor of Peoria, Illinois, accounts for most of our exports. With sales of $8.6 billion in 1980, Caterpillar dominates the industry as thoroughly as IBM dominates computers. Caterpillar is America's third-largest exporter, trailing only Boeing and General Electric.

Other major American construction machinery manufacturers include International Harvester, with construction machinery sales of $760 million in 1980; J.I. Case, a division of the diversified energy company Tenneco, with construction and agricultural machinery sales of $2.4 billion; John Deere, with construction machinery sales of $981 million; and Clark Equipment, with sales of $565 million.

All of these companies are being challenged by Komatsu of Japan, the world's second-largest manufacturer of earth-moving equipment, with 1980 sales of $2.2 billion. The company currently supplies 15 percent of all construction machinery sold in the world and is especially strong in the fast-growing markets of the Middle East, Southeast Asia, and South America.

Komatsu's goal is to become the leading construction machinery manufacturer in the world. The company's unofficial motto is "Maru-C," which means "Encircle Caterpillar." One way in which it hopes to carry through with this strategy is to establish itself in the United States market. Currently, it sells only tractors and loaders here, and has captured approximately 8 and 5 percent of these markets. In the 1980s, the firm hopes to increase these percentages significantly and also begin selling other equipment here. It is already building an extensive dealer network in the United States—between 1975 and 1980, Komatsu signed fifty-seven dealers to market its equipment. However, this still falls far short of Caterpillar's 106. Moreover, Cat's dealers sell only Caterpillar products, while Komatsu's distributors sell a whole range of competitors' equipment.

To attract customers, Komatsu is trying to price 10 to 15 percent below Caterpillar. The Japanese company is also offering larger and more electronically sophisticated machinery. A 720 horsepower hydraulic excavator unveiled in 1981 has twice the horsepower of Caterpillar's biggest machine, and Komatsu's 1000 horsepower tractor-bulldozer has 300 more horsepower than Cat's largest tractor. Komatsu's products will also come equipped with an electronic recording of a woman's voice to warn operators that the engine is overheating.

Komatsu is said to be considering the possibility of acquiring an American construction machinery firm, a quick way for them to start manufacturing operations here. Ocean freight charges from Japan on big earthmovers can add 10 percent or more to final costs. If Komatsu begins building equipment here, it will be able to price even more aggressively.

A foreign competitor that has already bought into the United States market is IBH Holding of West Germany, a conglomerate pieced together from ten European construction machinery manufacturers by a West German entrepreneur named Horst Dieter Esch. In 1980, Esch added to his holdings by purchasing General Motors' construction machinery division, TEREX, thus giving IBH a strong manufacturing base and distribution network in the United States.

IBH appears to be well positioned to increase its market share in the 1980s. The firm's sales have already increased from just $200 million in 1979 to over $1 billion in 1981. The company has been especially strong in Europe—Esch claims to have increased IBH's European market share by 5 percent in 1980 alone.

While the objective of both Komatsu and IBH is to take sales from Caterpillar, the firms that will be hurt the most are the second-tier American manufacturers. Some of them are already suffering—International Harvester's sales of construction machinery in 1980 were less than in 1975. Although this was primarily caused by a construction recession in the United States brought on by high interest rates, foreign competition was also an important factor. For the year, the firm lost nearly $400 million and was headed for another loss in 1981. Clark Equipment's sales of construction machinery were down $100 million in 1980, and John Deere's sales of earthmoving equipment were also down.

Signs of an incipient decline in construction machinery are thus becoming evident. Over the most recent five-year period, 1975 to 1980, imports of construction machinery grew faster than exports. America's trade balance can ill afford any further losses in this important industry.

Part Six

Early Casualties

28 Made in Japan, Taiwan, and Singapore

In the 1960s, consumer electronics was dominated by such American companies as RCA and General Electric. Today the Japanese and NICs control what has become a truly global market. Radios are made in South Korea, microwave ovens in Singapore, television sets in Taiwan, digital watches in Hong Kong, and video cassette recorders in Japan. These products are then exported all over the world.

Of the $11 billion worth of consumer electronic products sold in the United States in 1980, nearly half were manufactured abroad. Imports comprise 100 percent of all table radios sold here, 100 percent of all video recorders, 90 percent of CB radios, 85 percent of black and white televisions, 68 percent of digital watches, 64 percent of hi-fi components, 50 percent of electronic calculators, 43 percent of phonographs, and 33 percent of microwave ovens. As a result of all these imports, we ran a $3.7 billion trade deficit in consumer electronic products in 1980.

The speed with which the United States lost control of its consumer electronics market is astonishing. Of the more than 9 million radios sold in the United States in 1950, only 2,000 were imports. Ten years later, the market had expanded to 18 million sets, of which 7.5 million were made by foreign companies. In the early 1960s, the market reached 30 million sets with imports accounting for 80 percent. By the late 1970s, when the market reached 35 million radios, imports had captured the entire market. Although Japanese manufacturers were the first to send radios to the United States, they soon fell behind low-wage NICs like Hong Kong, Taiwan, Singapore, and South Korea. More than 50 percent of the radios currently imported into the United States are made in Hong Kong.

The experience with radios was repeated with black and white television sets. In 1960, imports accounted for less than 2,000 of the nearly 6 million televisions sold here. By 1970, the number of imports had increased 1,000 times to more than 2 million sets. By the end of the decade, more than 6 million black and white units were being imported into the United States each year, accounting for approximately 85 percent of the $500 million market.

The same trend is now visible in the color television market. Retail sales of color sets in the United States totaled more than $3.5 billion in 1980. Only recently dismissed as a mature, slow-growth market (sales leveled off at 10 million sets a year in 1978 and remained constant through 1980), color television is now poised for a boom decade. Analysts predict that the market might expand by as much as 50 percent by 1985.

The reason for this optimism is that the television has become the focal point for a variety of home entertainment systems. Cable TV has made it possible for viewers to tune in twenty or more different channels. Home Box Office brings second-run movies into the home. A new generation of electronic equipment, including videocassette recorders, videodisc players, video games, and home computers all utilize the television screen. As a result of these new options, demand for television sets has increased. Many families are buying a second or even a third color set. More than 85 percent of American households now own at least one color set and 40 percent have two or more. American television manufacturers once dreamed of a time when every household would own a color set; they now envision the day when each individual will have one. The catch of course is that the TV may be from Japan, Taiwan, or Korea.

Imports of Japanese-made color televisions to the United States began in the early 1970s and reached a high point of more than 2 million sets in 1976. American manufacturers, finding their market share dwindling and profits shrinking from foreign pressure, sought help from the federal government. The result was a so-called orderly marketing agreement in 1977 that limited imports to 1.5 million sets a year.

As Japanese exports slowed, Taiwanese and South Korean firms decided to make their move. Imports from Taiwan increased from 142,587 units in 1975 to 624,019 units in 1978. South Korean imports increased from 21,774 units to 437,000 units during the same period. American manufacturers were no more successful in beating back this invasion than they had been with the Japanese. Once again they turned to Washington for help. As a result, both Taiwan and South Korea were pressured into signing orderly marketing agreements that limited their imports to 373,000 and 153,000 units respectively. This, in turn, opened the market for Singapore, which exported 85,405 color sets in 1979.

Even with these import restrictions, the foreign onslaught continued. Japanese and Taiwanese firms decided to expand their manufacturing within the United States. Sony had previously constructed an assembly plant in San Diego in 1971. Matsushita followed by acquiring the TV production assets of Motorola (now Quasar) in 1974. Sanyo then bought Warwick Electronics in 1976. After the orderly marketing agreement was signed, Matsushita, Sharp, Hitachi, and Toshiba all opened plants here. As a result, approximately 3 million Japanese sets were manufactured within the United States during 1980. The largest producers were Sony,

Sanyo, and Quasar (Matsushita), each of which produced more than 750,000 sets. Taiwanese firms are now beginning to manufacture television sets here as well.

All this competition took a heavy toll on domestic producers. Of the more than twenty-five American color television manufacturers in the 1960s, only ten remained by 1981, and five of these were owned by foreign companies. Only three American producers are still major factors in the market: RCA, Zenith, and General Electric.

In the early 1960s, RCA controlled more than 65 percent of the domestic color television market. Most of the rest was divided between Zenith and Admiral. Today, RCA and Zenith each retain only a 20 percent market share. Admiral's facilities have been shut down. Close on the heels of RCA and Zenith is North American Philips Corporation, a division of the multibillion-dollar electronic giant N.V. Philips of The Netherlands. With its acquisition of Sylvania and Philco in addition to a prior acquisition of Magnavox, Philips controls about 15 percent of the American market. General Electric trails in fourth place with less than 8 percent of sales.

Although no single Japanese company has more than 10 percent of our market, eight Japanese companies together account for more than one-third of sales. On a worldwide basis, five Japanese companies rank among the top ten television manufacturers. RCA and Zenith are the only American companies left on this list. Matsushita alone manufactures nearly twice as many televisions as RCA and Zenith combined.

What has caused our decline in color televisions? Why have American producers fared so poorly against foreign competition? At least initially, Japanese manufacturers gained a foothold in the United States by resorting to unfair trading practices. Japanese companies such as Hitachi, Sanyo, and Mitsubishi (along with American distributors such as Sears, J. C. Penney, and Montgomery Ward) were found guilty of "dumping" television sets—selling them for less than the Japanese retail price. The Treasury Department imposed fines of $150 million—later reduced to $75 million—against these companies for import violations between 1971 and 1979. But the action came too late. The damage had been done.

Dumping is just one of the problems American companies have had to confront. The technology required to design and manufacture sets is no longer protected by patents and is readily understood and implemented in low-wage countries. Both radio and television assembly are very labor intensive. In 1970, when Japanese imports were beginning to flow into this country, Japanese labor costs were only one-half of ours. While Japanese labor costs have now risen to our level, wages in Taiwan, South Korea, and Singapore remain much lower.

Wage rates are not the whole story, however. American manufacturers could have tried to offset their labor disadvantage by aggressively automating, investing for productivity, and otherwise making the most of their high-volume production. They could also have stepped up investment in research and development to remain at the forefront of television technology. They chose not to take any of these steps, however, primarily because of short-term profit considerations.

Japanese manufacturers have automated manufacturing facilities to a much greater extent than have U.S. companies. By 1978, the hourly wage rate for manufacturing televisions had reached the same level in Japan and the United States, but because of automation, it still costs Japanese firms only about one half as much to manufacture a television set. The average time required to assemble a color set is just 1.9 hours in Japan versus 3.5 to 4.5 hours in the United States.

Japanese firms have outspent their American counterparts on research and development as well. According to the Northwestern University Center for the Interdisciplinary Study of Science and Technology, Japanese television manufacturers spent approximately 3.5 percent of their total sales on R&D in 1978 while American firms spent only 2.3 percent. Sony devoted 5.8 percent of its sales to R&D versus 2.3 percent for RCA.

Healthy research and development expenditures have enabled the Japanese to build better television sets. A study of mid-sized color televisions by *Consumer Reports* rated the following five televisions as best in their size range and equal in overall quality: MGA (Japanese), J.C. Penney's (made by RCA), RCA, Sanyo, and Sony. Japanese excellence in television manufacturing is also confirmed by repair records. According to *Consumer Reports,* Sony and Hitachi mid-sized color televisions require "fewer repairs" than other models in the same size range. MGA and Sanyo also had a better than average record. American models, on the other hand, were found to need more servicing than average.

Japanese television manufacturers are also actively developing new designs and features. These include stereo television and television with a second channel simultaneously projected in black and white in the righthand corner of the screen. Toshiba and Panasonic recently demonstrated a television that is activated by voice. Panasonic offers a television with a talking clock.

The Japanese are especially active in developing television components. As in today's stereo systems, accessories for television sets in the future will be priced and sold separately from the basic receivers. Customers will be able to upgrade their systems without buying new sets. Introduced in 1980 in Japan, Sony's component line accounted for nearly 20 percent of the firm's television sales.

Unless American manufacturers begin to respond to this technological challenge, the color television market will soon be lost in its entirety. Only thirty years were required to eliminate American companies from the radio business. The struggle for color television is now ten years old.

29 The Last Stand

Radio and television are not the only products that American consumer electronic manufacturers have let slip away, for U.S. firms have also lost the fast-growing markets for digital watches, microwave ovens, and video recorders to foreign competition. A brief look at our collapse in these products should help us to prepare for the coming battle in the videodisc market—our last chance to salvage a major piece of the consumer electronics industry.

Digital watches were supposed to be a bonanza for the United States. Because of our leadership in semiconductor technology—from which the digital watch was developed—it was thought that American firms would dominate the market. *Business Week* reported in 1975 that "there's no doubt that the digital watch will bring the watch business to the U.S."

Five years later, the same magazine ran a story that documented the demise of American digital watch manufacturers. Such major semiconductor companies as Fairchild Camera & Instrument, Intel, Litronix and Motorola had been driven from the business. Even Texas Instruments, which pioneered much of the digital watch technology, had run into trouble.

American digital watch manufacturers have been battered on two fronts. Japanese companies such as Seiko and Citizen quickly emulated Texas Instruments' basic technology and advanced it further by adding calendars, alarms, stopwatches, and calculators. These additions proved to be attractive to American consumers and gained the Japanese a major part of the medium- and high-priced market. At the other end of the market, U.S. manufacturers fell victim to Hong Kong. Assembling watches is a labor-intensive business, and Hong Kong has been able to exploit its advantage of relatively low cost labor. In 1979, the Crown Colony assembled some 40 million digital watches—more than one-half of total world sales. In total, nearly 70 percent of all digital watches sold in the United States are imports.

Microwave ovens now seem headed down the same path. The idea of using microwaves to cook food was first developed in the 1940s by a scientist at the Massachusetts-based firm Raytheon. Such ovens were confined to commercial uses until the late 1960s when Amana Refrigeration, a subsidiary of Raytheon, introduced the first countertop microwave oven. It took a while for the idea to catch on, but when it did, sales skyrocketed from 60,000 units in 1976 to 3.0 million in 1980. Analysts expect the market will double again by 1985, reaching nearly $3 billion in total sales. At present, fewer than one in five American households are equipped with a microwave oven. By the middle of the 1980s, it is expected that one of every two will have one.

Given our initial edge in microwave technology, one would have expected American manufacturers to prosper during this boom period. Instead, they faltered under the crush of Japanese exports. Japanese companies have already captured one-third of the American market for countertop ovens. Seven major Japanese firms—Hitachi, Matsushita, Mitsubishi, Riccar, Sanyo, Sharp, and Toshiba—together shipped more than 750,000 ovens to the United States in 1978.

Cut-rate Japanese prices have sent the profits of American manufacturers plummeting. The average profitability of the industry between 1976 and 1979 fell by 80 percent. One American producer, Micro Electronics Appliances, Inc., has already been forced out of business.

Unable to deal with the Japanese on their own, American microwave manufacturers sought government help. Sounding a familiar cry, they charged that the Japanese were dumping microwave ovens in an effort to seize the market. An investigation conducted by the United States International Trade Commission, however, concluded that only one Japanese manufacturer, Toshiba, was guilty of dumping; the others had gained their market share through fair competition.

The International Trade Commission noted that Sears, which sells microwave ovens under its own name, dropped its domestic supplier in favor of Sanyo because service calls "were two to three times higher" on the domestic models than on Japanese units. The commission also reported that Montgomery Ward dropped its domestic supplier in favor of Sharp because of "the firm's unsatisfactory experience with the quality of ovens procured from its U.S. supplier and the inability of its U.S. supplier to supply ovens with the features Ward believed were required."

Consumer Reports confirmed claims that the Japanese made better ovens. Their March 1981 edition contained an analysis of twenty-three of the most popular countertop microwave ovens sold here. Of that group, three Japanese products, one sold under the J.C. Penney's name, received the highest rating.

Having established a strong base, the Japanese are now moving to exploit their advantage. Matsushita, Sanyo, and Sharp all began manufacturing ovens here in 1979. Toshiba is currently building a plant and other Japanese manufacturers will likely follow.

Because of these new plants, Japanese imports began to taper off in 1979. Total imports of microwave ovens increased, however, as Singapore emerged as a major producer of countertop ovens. Imports from Singapore increased tenfold in one year alone, from approximately 10,000 units in 1978 to more than 100,000 in 1979.

American manufacturers can expect other NICs to enter the market as well. Unless American manufacturers respond soon with high-quality ovens and fully competitive prices, we will lose another once-promising business.

Video recorders represent yet another American failure in consumer electronics. This market has grown rapidly in the United States to an estimated million units in 1981. On a worldwide level, nearly 3 million units were sold in 1980, and sales should exceed 6 million a year by 1985.

Although the technology behind video recorders was long available to American television manufacturers, the Japanese were the first to develop it commercially. Sony introduced its Betamax model in 1976. Two years later, Japan Victor Corporation developed an alternative model called the Video Home System (VHS). VHS is similar to Betamax except that it uses slightly larger cassettes that are incompatible with Betamax. Today Matsushita, Sanyo, and Toshiba also produce video recorders. No American firms are yet manufacturing these machines. RCA and General Electric are buying their video recorders from Matsushita, while Zenith has relied on Sony.

Our last chance to salvage a major piece of the consumer electronics industry lies in videodiscs. Videodisc technology promises to reshape the consumer electronics industry in the same way that television did when it was first introduced. A videodisc looks like a long-playing record, and is played on a machine that looks and works much like a phonograph. Connected to a television, the videodisc player makes it possible to view prerecorded movies and shows. Unlike a video recorder, it cannot tape directly from the screen, but it costs only about half as much as a video recorder, and videodiscs cost an average of $20 versus $40 for a prerecorded tape.

The videodisc market is expected to grow very rapidly. Analysts believe that disc sales will eventually outpace the sales of color television sets. The market for the players alone is expected to exceed 5 million units a year by 1990. The battle for this multibillion-dollar business will be intense. Three different video systems have been developed by Philips, RCA, and Matsushita, all of which are incompatible with one another.

The Philips system, designed in conjunction with Japan's Pioneer Electronic Corporation, the world's largest seller of stereo equipment, was first on the market. It uses sophisticated optical laser technology and is being sold in the United States under the Magnavox name. The system was listed for sale at $750 in 1981, but could be purchased at some discount stores for under $600. The Philips system offers such extra features as the ability to play in stereo, freeze frames, and play discs at various speeds.

RCA spent nearly $200 million to develop its videodisc system, which it began marketing in the spring of 1981. The RCA system uses more conventional technology, does not include the extras of the Philips system, and sold for under $500 in 1981. RCA executives hope that the low price of their machine will make it a bestseller. The company has also enlisted a formidable group of allies to push its machine. Zenith, Sanyo, Hitachi, Toshiba, and Radio Shack have all signed contracts to manufacture RCA-type players and sell them under their own names.

Matsushita's disc player, which the company will market under its National, Panasonic, and Quasar brand names, was scheduled to be on the market by the end of 1981. The Matsushita system operates with technology similar to RCA's, but includes many of the extras offered by the Philips laser player. The Matsushita machine is expected to sell for about $500. Matsushita has signed an agreement with General Electric, which will build and market videodisc players of Matsushita's design.

Because all three machines will probably sell within $100 of each other, a major factor in the consumer's purchasing decision will be the available entertainment package. With system incompatibility, the competition to secure good programming is intense. Philips has struck a deal with MCA, Inc., the giant entertainment conglomerate that owns Universal Studios; RCA has contracted with CBS; and Matsushita with Thorn EMI, Ltd., owner of Capitol Records. The firm that puts together the best entertainment package will give its manufacturing partner a significant advantage.

Applications of videodisc technology will not be confined to consumer electronics. Videodiscs will have a place in the computer industry as well. Using the more advanced laser technology pioneered by Philips, computer companies hope to be able to engrave both data and images on plastic discs for storage. Toshiba is already marketing an electronic file cabinet that stores data in this manner. The Toshiba system records 10,000 documents on a single disc that costs less than $150. Philips has developed an experimental disc capable of storing the entire Encyclopaedia Britannica.

The consumer electronics industry thus reaches far beyond itself—over the next several decades, it will interact with semiconductors, computers, and telecommunications. As a Northwestern University study pointed out: "Consumer electronics is central to our system of mass communications and culture. Projected expansion into such areas as education, energy management, security, and information processing will intensify this centrality. It is one of this nation's important reservoirs of technology and technical skills; it has important potential links to military technology. It is an important part of the structure of industry."

To lose consumer electronics entirely to the Japanese and the NICs would weaken our entire economy and cast doubt on our future as an economic power. Videodisc technology represents our last stand. If we can win this market, we will have secured for ourselves a central position in the consumer electronics industry for years to come.

30 Nippon Steel

At the end of World War Two, the United States was preeminent in steel. We manufactured nearly 50 percent of the world's output and supplied 15 percent of the world's exports.

The era of American dominance was, however, destined to be short-lived. Although steel became one of the first international markets, American steel executives were not accustomed to thinking in international terms, nor were they accustomed to competition.

For years, the steel industry had competed in a sheltered market. Prices were set by industry leaders—U.S. Steel and Bethlehem Steel. One of these monoliths would announce a price increase and everyone else would follow. Smaller competitors who might have been tempted to cut prices slightly in order to gain market share were kept in line by the fear that the industry giants would "punish" them by drastically cutting prices and driving them out of business. As a result of this quasi-monopoly pricing strategy, the industry became increasingly complacent.

In the immediate postwar period, American steel could have expanded all around the world by taking advantage of its size and its then modern plants. But this would have meant competing aggressively by reducing prices and would have had a negative impact on short-term profits and stock prices. The easier course was simply to let foreign competition multiply along with domestic. In the short run at least, this saved the industry billions of dollars that otherwise would have had to be invested in new plant and equipment. In the long run, however, this strategy led to near ruin.

By the mid-1950s, American steel had already embarked on a downward slide from which it would never recover. Between 1955 and 1980, steel production in the rest of the world increased five times faster than in the United States. American firms fell steadily behind in market share and eventually lost all the advantages of size and mass production with which they had started. By 1980 our once favorable trade balance in steel had been reversed. Instead of the world's largest steel exporter, we became the world's largest importer. Imports exceeded exports by $4.2 billion and accounted for 16 percent of all steel sold in the U.S. that year.

This declining competitiveness came to national attention in the late 1970s. In 1977, Bethlehem Steel, the nation's second-largest steel manufacturer, reported losses of $477 million. Subsequently the firm was forced to shut down two large steel plants in Johnstown, Pennsylvania, and in Lackawanna, New York, laying off 10,000 workers in the process. Another producer, Youngstown Sheet and Tube, closed its plants near Youngstown, Ohio, in the same year, and laid off 5,000 workers. In 1979, U.S. Steel shut down thirteen plants, putting 13,000 people out of work. The company reported a loss of $504 million for the year.

As American steel power waned, a host of other countries benefited. The biggest winner, however, was "Japan, Inc." Between 1950 and 1980, Japanese steel production rose from 5 to 111 million metric tons. During this period Japan's share of the world steel market increased from 3 to 17 percent.

Today, four of the ten largest steel companies in the world are Japanese. Only two American companies, U.S. Steel and Bethlehem, remain on the list; the other four are located in Western Europe. Nippon Steel has long since replaced U.S. Steel as the world's largest steel manufacturer. The Japanese have not only been able to master and improve the manufacturing technology originally pioneered by American companies, but have been able to achieve a competitive cost advantage of at least 20 percent.

There are several reasons for the Japanese cost advantage, but a major factor is labor. Steelworkers in the United States are represented by one of the country's most powerful unions, the United Steel Workers (USW), which represents 1.4 million workers and has accumulated net assets of $117 million. The union has used its strength to win large wage gains. Between 1970 and 1980, employment costs in the industry increased by more than 300 percent. The average hourly compensation in the steel industry in 1980 was $19, which is 60 percent more than in other manufacturing industries in the United States and approximately 100 percent more than Japanese steelworkers earn.

Such a wage differential could be supported only by a highly automated and productive industry. The American steel industry is neither. Productivity increases in the industry lagged behind other American manufacturing industries by nearly 50 percent between 1957 and 1975. International comparisons are even more striking. Over the same period, output per person per hour in Japanese steel manufacturing increased by 166 percent, in Western Europe by 89 percent, and in the U.S. by 17 percent.

A major reason for this dismal record is that management has failed to make necessary capital investments. The Japanese have far more modern plant and equipment. In the last fifteen years, they have built nine massive new steel complexes, compared to one medium-size plant constructed in the U.S.

American steel plants are much less modern than Japanese facilities and they are also technologically deficient. There have been two major technological breakthroughs in steel manufacturing in recent years: the basic oxygen furnace and a process called continuous casting. U.S. steel companies trail the competition in adopting both.

The basic oxygen furnace (BOF) replaced the open hearth furnace as the most efficient way to produce steel. The BOF is less expensive to build and to operate. Despite this, American steel companies have been slow to change from the open hearth process because of the initial conversion costs. By the mid-1970s, over 80 percent of all steel produced in Japan was made with BOF, versus 70 percent in West Germany and only 60 percent here.

Management has also been slow to adopt continuous casting, a process first developed in West Germany in the 1950s. Continuous casting simplifies production by condensing several separate operations into one. This has improved both productivity and the quality of the steel produced. The process can save more than 50 percent of the energy previously used in the same stages of steel production. The Japanese have been quick to see these advantages—more than 65 percent of their steel was made by this method in 1980. In Western Europe, the figure was 43 percent. But only 18 percent of American steel was produced this way.

Aside from newer and more technologically advanced plants, Japanese steel companies also benefit from larger plants. This is important because of the tremendous economies of scale available in steel manufacturing. In general, the larger the size of a steel plant, the lower the average cost of production will be. The ten largest Japanese steel plants have an average production capacity of 11.5 million metric tons, compared to 5.9 for the ten largest American counterparts.

A final factor explaining the lack of competition of American steel manufacturers is government regulation. In this country, steel companies must fight through a

maze of federal, state, and local regulations. The Council
of Wage and Price Stability under President Carter
counted over 5,600 separate federal regulations govern-
ing the steel industry, and this figure excludes state and
local regulations. Most of these regulations concern pollution control, and the cost of meeting them can be substantial. By the mid-1970s, approximately 20 percent of
all capital spending in the steel industry was devoted to
meeting pollution standards.

The direct cost of complying with the regulations is
not, however, the principal problem. According to the
Federal Trade Commission, Japanese steel companies
spend more on pollution control equipment than U.S.
companies do. The problem with government regulations—at least as they pertain to steel—is that they are
confusing and create uncertainty. Regulations at the
local, state, and federal level are often inconsistent with
one another or even contradictory. There is no single
agency or person authorized to resolve conflicts, so the
result can be very time consuming and expensive. As the
Council on Wage and Price Stability emphasized: "The
industry faces significant uncertainty about the specific
air and water quality standards which it must meet. In
most cases, these involve continued litigation and negotiation with state and federal regulatory on a plant-by-
plant basis." The problem is thus not so much the regulations as the regulators.

The Japanese do not face this. Business and government have worked closely together to formulate a set of
regulations that are as rigorous as those in the United
States, but are much easier to understand and adminis-
ter. The Japanese steel industry and government have a
long history of cooperation. After World War Two, the
Japanese government gave top priority to the development of the steel industry and instructed the Ministry of
International Trade and Industry to devise a plan for the
industry's development. MITI responded with what has

come to be known as the First Rationalization Plan, which articulated two strategic goals: to increase productivity through the use of the latest technology and to achieve economies of scale through industry consolidation.

The government worked closely with the country's financial institutions to ensure that the steel companies got the funds needed to enact the MITI plan. In fact, the government-supported Reconstruction Bank of Japan became the largest creditor for the development program. The government further aided steel through tax benefits and import restrictions. Perhaps most importantly, they relaxed antitrust laws to permit a merger between the two largest steel companies, Yawata and Fuji Steel. The new company was renamed Nippon Steel.

Government support was essential in launching the Japanese steel industry. Once MITI's initial goals were accomplished, however, its aid was withdrawn and Japanese companies were left to fend for themselves in world markets. The result has been a rout of the competition.

31 Trigger Prices

Faced with the Japanese onslaught, American steel companies eventually turned to Washington for help. Steel executives charged that their industry was being victimized by the tendency of foreign producers to dump steel in our markets.

The Anti-Dumping Act of 1921, as amended by the Trade Act of 1977, made it illegal for foreigners to dump their excess production in the United States by selling it at prices below those charged in the home market or at prices below cost (plus an allowance made for profit). In 1977, U.S. Steel filed a massive antidumping suit against Japanese manufacturers while National Steel and Armco filed similar suits against European steel firms.

Worried that such suits might precipitate a trade war, the Carter Administration intervened and offered the industry price protection in exchange for dropping the suits. The steel companies agreed. The Carter aid plan was based on trigger prices. As defined by the Treasury Department, a trigger price is "a standard price level for selling imported steel, below which sales would be investigated for dumping violations." This minimum selling price is based on estimates of the production costs of the Japanese—deemed by the Treasury to be the world's most efficient steel manufacturers. Any manufacturer found guilty of dumping faces a stiff penalty.

Whatever their initial purpose, trigger prices have come to be a means of artificially supporting the price of steel in order to subsidize the inefficiency of our steel manufacturers. While supposedly based on Japanese production costs, trigger prices have been raised in an arbitrary manner. As a result, steel prices increased from $431 per metric ton in 1978 to $518 in 1980.

Even with higher prices, however, the American producers continued to have problems. Profit levels remained depressed. Consequently, in March 1980, U.S. Steel filed another antidumping suit, this one directed at steel producers in seven Western European nations. The Carter Administration again responded with an agreement to raise the level of trigger prices in exchange for withdrawal of the suit.

As the debate over dumping and trigger prices has waxed and waned, the underlying weaknesses of the American industry have not been addressed. Labor costs remain very high and little is being done to bring them into line with other manufacturing industries. In 1980, the steel companies and the United Steel Workers agreed to a contract that will raise labor costs by 34 percent over a three-year period.

Nor has the industry yet made a full commitment to modern plant and equipment. It is estimated that building a new medium-size, fully integrated steel works in the United States would require seven to ten years and cost $5 billion or more. Given the industry outlook, it is unlikely that any manufacturer is going to want to put that much money into steel. Indeed, most American steel manufacturers are doing all they can to diversify away from the industry. By contrast, Japan's Nippon Kokan recently completed what is being called the world's most sophisticated steel mill at a cost of $4 billion.

In the long run, however, even the Japanese may be hard pressed to preserve their domestic steel industries. All the industrialized nations are threatened by steel imports from South Korea, Taiwan, Singapore, Mexico, and Brazil. These countries enjoy both modern facilities—usually subsidized by their governments—and low labor costs of $2 per hour in Southeast Asia and $4 per

hour in South America. The NICs have been able to capitalize on these advantages to achieve a rapid growth rate
in steel production. Between 1970 and 1978, South
American and Southeast Asian steel production increased at an annual rate of 7.6 percent and 11.3 percent, compared to 0.5 percent in the United States and
1.1 percent in Japan. As Brookings Institute economist
Robert Solomon has noted: "No matter what the U.S.
does, the steel business will probably drift to the
NICs."

South Korea is a prime example of an emerging steel
power. National steel production increased from 476,000
metric tons in 1970 to 8.5 million in 1980. Pohang Iron
and Steel has constructed one of the largest and most
modern steel works in the world and plans a second facility. It is already selling steel in Korea for 25 percent less
than the Japanese charge in their home market.

Closer to home, Mexico is becoming a formidable
challenger in the North and South American steel markets. Mexican steelworkers earn about one-fourth as
much as their counterparts in the United States and their
productivity is rapidly rising to the American level. Mexican steel companies have been quick to adopt the latest
manufacturing techniques. Hysla, the largest steel manufacturer, has innovated a process known as "direct
reduction" which produces significant cost savings.

Even the poorer developing countries such as Indonesia, Nigeria, and Zambia are beginning to manufacture
their own steel. The number of steel-producing nations in
the world has more than doubled since 1950 and more
entrants can be expected in the future. By the turn of the
century, any country with a semiskilled labor force will
be producing steel. For many of the less developed countries, it is a matter of national pride to have a steel company. These companies will be unable to compete in the
international marketplace at first, but will be subsidized
and protected by their governments.

As more and more nations enter the global steel industry, American manufacturers with high-cost labor and out-of-date plants will find it increasingly difficult to compete. Today's trigger prices will probably not hold up. Eventually, our steel prices will be so out of line with the rest of the world that it will threaten our competitiveness in other industries. Already, according to another Brookings economist, Robert Crandall, American steel consumers are paying more than $1 billion per year to subsidize our domestic steel producers. At some point, American companies forced to pay artificially high prices for steel will not be able to compete with foreign competitors able to buy steel in the global marketplace. When this happens, trigger prices will collapse and reality will finally have to be faced.

32 From Riches to Rags

In 1978, the American automobile industry seemed to be in robust health. General Motors' annual report began with the statement that "1978 was a year of extraordinary achievement—by many measures, the best in our history." The company had sold nearly 10 million cars worldwide and reported a profit of more than $3.5 billion. Ford also enjoyed record sales in 1978 and a profit of more than $1.5 billion, and even financially troubled American Motors managed to make money.

Only the performance of Chrysler Corporation hinted that anything was remotely wrong with the industry. Chrysler reported losses for the year of $200 million. Despite this setback, management remained optimistic about the firm's future, assuring shareholders that better days were coming.

The following year, however, the company lost a staggering $1.1 billion, at that time the largest loss ever reported by an American company, and to save the firm from bankruptcy, the federal government guaranteed $1.5 billion in loans. Nor was Chrysler the only automobile manufacturer with problems in 1979. Ford's North American motor vehicle operations lost more than $1 billion. Only the company's success in Europe allowed it to report a profit for the year.

The industry took yet another turn for the worse in 1980. Chrysler reported another record loss of $1.7 billion, Ford followed close behind with $1.5 billion, and American Motors, newly rescued from financial collapse by the French auto giant Renault, lost nearly $200 mil-

lion. Even General Motors reported losses of more than
$700 million. It was the first time since the Great
Depression that GM had failed to earn a profit.

In only two years, the industry had sunk from prosperity to poverty. What had happened? Why had such a
proud industry, traditionally the bellwether of the entire
American economy, turned so swiftly into a disaster
area? For many industry analysts, the answer lay in the
Iranian Revolution. The shah's overthrow disrupted the
flow of Iranian oil and sent world oil prices soaring. The
price of gasoline at the pump increased from $.69 a gal-
lon in January 1979 to $1.22 by the beginning of 1980.

People reacted to this change by rushing to exchange
their GM, Ford, and Chrysler models for more gas-efficient foreign imports. In only one year, between January
1979 and January 1980, the mix of cars sold in the U.S.
shifted from 23 percent large cars, 33 percent medium-
size cars, and 40 percent small cars, to 14 percent large,
32 mid-sized, and 56 percent compact and subcompact.

American automobile manufacturers were unprepared
for this tidal change. For decades the American market
had been sheltered from foreign competition by consumer demand for big luxury cars. Manufacturers had
always emphasized selling profitable large cars at the
expense of small cars. According to a former GM executive's controversial account of the automobile industry,
On a Clear Day You Can See General Motors, the cost
of manufacturing a Chevrolet was just $300 less than the
cost of manufacturing a Cadillac. Yet the Cadillac sold
for $4000 more. Obviously, Detroit preferred to sell
Cadillacs rather than Chevys.

In the mid-1970s, Lee Iacocca, then president of Ford
Motor Company, suggested to Henry Ford that the company build a small, front-wheel-drive subcompact. The
idea was allegedly discarded because Ford felt the cost of
designing and building such a car would unduly depress

profits and hurt the company's stock price. As a result of such attitudes, Detroit failed to develop high-quality small cars.

By contrast, Japanese and European automobile manufacturers had become specialists in small cars. In 1979, foreign manufacturers offered four times as many compact and subcompact models in the U.S. market as American manufacturers. The Environmental Protection Agency's ratings on gas mileage showed that eighteen of the twenty most fuel-efficient automobiles on the American market were imports. The two "American" cars listed in the top twenty, the Dodge Colt and the Plymouth Champ, were actually built in Japan. Both Japanese and European companies were thus well positioned to capitalize on soaring gas prices.

Events in Iran certainly boosted the sales of Japanese and European cars. At the same time, the downfall of the shah is not sufficient to explain the magnitude of the decline of the American automobile industry. A more thoughtful analysis suggests that the troubles began as early as the 1950s. Since the mid-1950s, virtually all the growth in new car sales in the United States has been taken by foreign imports. In 1955, they represented less than one percent of new cars sold here. By 1981 this figure had increased to almost 30 percent. As a group, foreign manufacturers have surpassed Ford and assumed the number-two place in the American market.

As in the consumer electronics industry, it is the Japanese who are supplying the great majority of the imports. Just twenty-five years ago, Japanese automobile production was only one percent of American. Since then it has increased 25,000 times, while our production has remained stagnant. In 1980, Japan became the largest producer of automobiles in the world.

Japan is also the world's number-one exporter. Each year approximately 50 percent of its domestic production is shipped abroad. New car sales are Japan's largest single source of foreign exchange, earning the nation some $17.5 billion in 1979, and nearly half of these earnings came from the United States.

Our long-term decline relative to Japan can be traced to some of the same factors that have led to the downfall of the consumer electronics industry. Perhaps the most basic problem is that automotive technology used in the United States today is no longer sufficiently advanced to support the high wage rates of American workers. According to the Department of Transportation's 1981 special report to the president on the U.S. automobile industry, the Japanese can build a car and ship it to the United States for $1,000 to $1,500 less than it costs an American manufacturer to build a car here. A major reason is the cost of labor. American autoworkers are among the best-paid workers in America and enjoy wages 50 percent higher than their counterparts in similar industries. According to the Department of Transportation, the average wage rate in the American automobile industry in 1979 exceeded $14 an hour, approximately double the Japanese equivalent.

Yet even if wage rates were equal, more than half the Japanese cost advantage would remain. The greater source of Japan's competitive advantage lies in its advanced manufacturing technology and higher productivity. Japanese companies in 1980 produced an average of forty-one cars per worker per year versus an average of twelve for the big three Detroit automakers.

Management must shoulder the blame for this poor record. American automobile manufacturers have failed to make the necessary investments to improve productivity. Japanese automobile assembly plants are the most automated in the world. At Nissan's Zama plant outside Tokyo, where Datsun cars are manufactured, computer controlled robots perform 96 percent of the required welding. Advanced automation of this kind allows the plant to turn out more than seventy cars a year per employee.

While American companies have steadily lost ground on the cost front, they have also slipped in product quality and innovation. As a result, the Japanese are now able to build better cars. Such innovations as front-wheel drive, four-cylinder engines, rotary engines, radial tires, disc brakes, seat and shoulder belts, rack-and-pinion steering, rear-window defoggers, sunroofs, and five-speed transmissions were either first introduced or first became standard equipment in Japanese cars.

A survey of Detroit automotive engineers conducted in 1980 by Montgomery Ward's *Auto World* magazine confirmed what is already obvious to most: Japanese cars are superior. Nearly 50 percent of the engineers who responded to the survey said that Japanese manufacturers produced the best-quality cars, while 27 percent voted for American manufacturers, and the rest for German companies.

Further evidence of Japanese technical superiority is provided by *Consumer Reports'* 1980 survey of new car repair records. Of the twenty-nine cars given the highest rating, all were foreign made (although three were sold by American companies). Of the twenty cars given the lowest rating, all were American made.

Department of Transportation statistics on recalls tell the same story. During the five-year period between 1974 and 1978, a total of 25 million motor vehicles produced by American Motors, Chrysler, Ford, General Motors, Honda, Nissan, Toyota, and Volkswagen were recalled to correct safety defects. American-made vehicles accounted for more than 24 million of them, or 96 percent! Ford had to recall more than 3.5 million motor vehicles in 1978 alone; in the same year, Nissan recalled a mere 389.

CONSUMER REPORTS REPAIR RECORDS
OF 1980 MODEL CARS

"Much better than average"	*"Much worse than average"*
Audi 4000	AMC Concord 6
Audi 5000	Buick Skylark 4
BMW 320i	Buick Skylark V6
Datsun 280X	Cadillac Eldorado
Datsun 210	Cadillac Seville
Datsun 310	Chevrolet Camaro V8
Datsun 510	Chevrolet Citation 4
Dodge Colt	Chevrolet Citation V6
Hatchback*	Chevrolet Corvette
Honda Accord	Chevrolet Monte
Honda Civic CVC	Carlo V8
Honda Civic	Chevrolet Monza 4
Honda Prelude	Chevrolet Nova 6
Mazda 626	Ford Mustang V6
Mazda GLC	Lincoln Continental
Mazda RX-7	Oldsmobile Omega 4
Mercedes Benz 240D	Oldsmobile Omega V6
Mercedes Benz 300D	Plymouth Volare 6
Plymouth Champ*	Pontiac Firebird V8
Renault Le Car	Pontiac Phoenix 4
Subaru	Pontiac Grand Prix V8
Toyota Celica	
Toyota Corolla	
Toyota Tercel	
Toyota Corona	
Toyota Cressida	
VW Dasher	
Volvo 4	
Volvo 6	

*Made in Japan

Another 10 million Ford automobiles were almost recalled because of a potentially dangerous transmission problem. When idling, these models sometimes jumped from park into reverse. The Center for Auto Safety, a consumer group, blames more than fifty deaths and 2,000 accidents on this problem. Ford has already recalled 1.5 million Pintos, whose gas tank was alleged to explode in rear-end collisions. The problem was corrected at a cost of nearly $40 million. In May of 1978, Chrysler recalled its Volare and Aspen models to correct front-end suspension faults that could cause loss of control of the automobiles. For some of these cars, it was their fourth recall in eight months.

As the American automobile industry entered the 1980s, it was thus producing a line of cars that cost more to buy and operate, but were not as well made as Japanese cars. Combined with record high interest rates and finance charges, these factors were producing a prolonged buyers' strike and a tide of red ink.

33 The $165 Billion Question

When the Reagan Administration entered the White House in January 1981, it immediately confronted the problem of the automobile industry. More than twenty major automobile plants across the country were closed. One quarter of a million autoworkers had been laid off.

The automobile depression threatened the entire economy. One out of every six jobs in the U.S. is tied to the motor vehicle industry in one way or another. Four million jobs are directly dependent on it. The industry consumes 25 percent of the nation's glass output, 21 percent of steel production, and 20 percent of machine tools, as well as significant percentages of plastics and electronics. Our automakers are among the largest companies in the world. Together they command assets of more than $165 billion. Their combined world sales came to more than $100 billion in 1980.

Given the size and importance of the industry, the Administration felt that it had to take steps to prevent further deterioration. After much discussion, a decision was made to seek "voluntary" import restrictions from Japan. Following a series of meetings between U.S. Trade Representative William Brock and Japanese officials, the restrictions were announced in May of 1981. Under the terms of a three-year agreement, Japan would reduce its automobile exports to the U.S. by 8 percent from a high of 1.82 million units in 1980 to 1.68 million units in both 1981 and 1982. The number of exports to be allowed here in 1983 was left for further negotiation.

The Administration hoped that this agreement would give the industry some time to regroup and make the changes needed to regain its lost competitiveness. The reality of the situation, however, is that import restrictions may only raise the price of Japanese cars. Similar restrictions have failed to revitalize the domestic color television and steel industries, and there are at least three reasons why they will probably also fail in the case of automobiles.

The first is that the Japanese can choose to manufacture cars in the United States instead of Japan. Honda, whose sales here have increased by more than 150 percent since 1976, is doing just that. The firm is spending $200 million to build a manufacturing plant in Marysville, Ohio, that should be turning out 10,000 cars a month by the end of 1982. Nissan is building a $400 million truck plant near Nashville, Tennessee, that is scheduled to begin producing 120,000 small pickup trucks a year in 1983. This plant may eventually be expanded to assemble cars as well. Toyota is also exploring the possibility of making cars here.

Second, just because Japanese imports are limited, it does not follow that American consumers will opt for American cars. Volkswagen is planning to make a major effort to increase its U.S. market share in the 1980s. VW captured almost 7 percent of the American market in the late 1960s with its low-priced Beetle, but in the mid-1970s, its market share fell sharply as the Deutschmark's appreciation against the dollar sent the price of the Beetle soaring. As a result, the company phased the Beetle out of its product line and introduced a new car, the highly successful Rabbit, today the world's best-selling car. To avoid further exchange rate problems, VW decided in 1978 to build the first foreign owned manufacturing plant on American soil in Westmoreland, Pennsylvania. The Westmoreland plant has been so successful that the company elected to build a second one outside Detroit, scheduled to be completed in the summer of 1982. With both plants operating, VW will have the capacity to produce 400,000 Rabbits a year. Further down the road, VW is hard at work planning its replacement for the Rabbit. Scheduled for production some time between 1986 and 1990, this new generation of cars will run on a revolutionary diesel engine that engineers hope will get more than seventy-five miles per gallon.

The French government-owned automaker Renault is also moving into the United States. In 1979, the firm announced it had reached a partnership agreement with financially ailing American Motors. Renault plans to build cars in AMC's factories and distribute them through AMC's extensive dealer network. Renault is potentially an even more dangerous foe than Volkswagen. In 1980, this firm enjoyed sales of over $20 billion and earned a healthy profit at a time when American and European competitors were losing money, a performance that enabled it to solidify its position as the leading manufacturer of automobiles in Europe.

Renault has achieved its success by designing a fleet of mechanically reliable cars that average more than thirty miles per gallon, the best performance of any European manufacturer. This is just the type of vehicle that will look attractive to American consumers if the supply of Japanese compacts and subcompacts becomes limited.

Using the financial resources of the French government, Renault has established itself as one of the leading users of automated technology in the world. Robots now perform nearly 40 percent of the work previously done by human beings on the assembly line. A spokesman for the company claims that Renault robotics is ahead of anything in Europe and the United States and certainly as good as anything in Japan.

A third factor working against the Reagan import restriction program is that it has come late—perhaps too late to save the industry. While General Motors will undoubtedly survive, Chrysler's and Ford's positions are much more tenuous.

Although Chrysler staged a rally in 1981, actually turning a profit for part of the year, the outlook remains grim. Standard & Poor's, a Wall Street firm that rates the creditworthiness of securities, has dropped the ratings on the company's bonds from B to CCC, the second-lowest possible rating where the highest is AAA. The CCC rating is defined as "predominantly speculative with respect to capacity to repay interest and repay principal."

In an effort to save the corporation, company officials have been trying to be acquired by or to merge with a large foreign automaker. In May of 1981, Chrysler's management announced that Peugeot had agreed to develop a new car for the U.S. market jointly with Chrysler. This alliance appears to be one of the blind leading the blind, for Peugeot has plenty of problems of its own. Its market share in France has been declining steadily since 1978, falling from 44 to 33 percent in 1981. In 1980, the firm lost $360 million and was headed for another loss in 1981.

Ford's troubles are almost as bad. Between 1978 and 1980, its domestic auto sales plunged 41 percent, and, as previously mentioned, the only thing that has prevented the company from becoming another Chrysler has been the success of its foreign operations. In Europe, Ford is the fifth-largest car distributor after Renault, Peugeot, Fiat, and VW. Even there, however, the company's market share is under pressure from increased Japanese imports. The lucrative West German market is a good illustration. Japanese car companies increased their market share in Germany from less than 2 percent in 1978 to 10 percent by the end of 1980. During this period, Ford's market share declined from 14 to 9 percent. In 1980, Ford's German operations lost $254 million. Japanese imports into Europe will undoubtedly increase further as American market growth is shut off.

If its European operations become a loser, Ford will

have to turn things around in the United States to avoid bankruptcy. Its chances ride on the success of its new front-wheel-drive "world cars," the Escort and Lynx. Ford spent approximately $1 billion developing these, yet even with an investment of this magnitude, it is not clear that the company can compete with the Japanese. The March 1981 issue of *Consumer Reports* presented the results of road tests conducted on the Escort, the Toyota Tercel, and Mazda GLC. The Escort received the lowest rating. The Japanese cars were also priced below the Ford—the Tercel's best price is approximately $700 less. Furthermore, Ford has already had to recall the Escort/Lynx seven times for minor safety defects.

Ford has other problems as well. The company was the last major manufacturer to convert from rear-wheel drive to more fuel efficient and spacious front-wheel-drive cars (shifting a car's steering controls from the back to the front both reduces the weight of the vehicle and creates more space in the rear). It will cost Ford nearly $30 billion and require as long as six years to market a complete line of front-wheel-drive cars—assuming that the company can raise the $30 billion. In 1980, the company increased its debt by $2.5 billion and saw its credit rating slashed by Standard & Poor's from AAA to A. As a result, it will be more difficult and expensive for Ford to raise the funds it so desperately needs. Without this cash, the company will slowly decay.

General Motors, which is still the largest manufacturer of automobiles in the world, remains our best hope for preserving an American position in the world automobile market. GM is spending some $40 billion to downsize and redesign its entire product line. This should be completed by 1985. The company introduced its first front-wheel-drive compact cars, the so-called X-cars, in 1980 and followed with its long-awaited J-car in 1981. The J-car is a front-wheel-drive subcompact that offers twenty-six miles to the gallon in the city and forty-three miles on the highway. Mid-sized A-cars were introduced in 1982. Still larger front-wheel-drive B-cars, C-cars, and a sporty P-car are scheduled to be unveiled in 1982 and 1983. By 1984, more than 90 percent of GM's products will feature front-wheel drive.

The company is also investing in robotics in order to automate assembly operations, for high wage rates remain a major problem. In 1981, the average list price of a GM car was over $10,000. Most new J-cars list between $7,000 and $9,000, and along with high financing charges, these prices have depressed early sales. The car could still prove to be a success, but if GM wants to remain competitive over the long run, it will have to cut costs significantly through automation.

Automation could help solve GM's quality control problems as well. The X-cars, which took four years and $2.7 billion to develop, have been a problem from the start. In their first year and a half on the road, they were recalled nine times for possible safety defects. *Consumer Reports* has judged all four X-car models, the Buick Skylark, Chevrolet Citation, Oldsmobile Omega, and Pontiac Phoenix to be "much worse than average" on needed repairs.

GM has another problem that automation cannot solve. The American automobile market is saturated. Nearly 90 percent of all households own at least one car and more than 50 percent own two or more. There is little room for the market to expand. During the ten-year period from 1968 to 1978, the average annual growth rate of the U.S. automobile market per 1,000 population was only 2.7 percent. This contrasted to Asian growth of 7.8 percent; South American of 7.0 percent; European of 5.2 percent; and African of 4.0 percent. Except for Europe, where the market is also becoming saturated, these trends should continue into the next decade.

Japanese firms are already positioned to exploit the fast-growing markets of the developing world. In 1980, their sales in Latin America increased 81 percent, in the Middle East 44 percent, in Southeast Asia 41 percent, and in Africa 32 percent. In total, Japanese manufacturers sold over 2 million cars in developing countries in 1980, and they also hope to exploit the potentially huge Chinese market, if and when it is opened to the outside world.

Western European manufacturers are also well established in the Third World. Volkswagen is the leading manufacturer in Brazil, the largest market in South America. French firms have used their former colonial ties to build a strong base in Africa. Peugeot has established a strong presence in Eastern Europe by manufacturing cars for Yugoslavia, Romania, and East Germany.

Juergen Donges, already mentioned as an expert in economic development at West Germany's Kiel Institute of World Economics, predicts that newly industrialized countries will also become significant competitors in the world automobile market. South Korea is already manufacturing its own cars and exporting them around the world, and Taiwan plans to become an automobile manufacturer, probably in cooperation with a Japanese company.

General Motors, which has never been a very aggressive or successful competitor outside the United States, will have to do better in the future if it wants to survive in the world automobile market. The very automation strategies that are the key to American survival in the automobile business require massive production volume to succeed. If Japanese, Western European, and even Third World companies continue to absorb virtually all the international growth, General Motors will become an ever higher cost producer and eventually may disappear from the market.

34 The Tools of Industry

Machine tools are used to cut and form metal. They drill, forge, grind, shape, saw, and weld. Worldwide production exceeded $26.5 billion in 1980, with the American market representing nearly one-fourth of the total.

The importance of the industry cannot be measured either by its sales or by the 100,000 jobs it provides American workers. Machine tools help determine the competitiveness of other industries such as construction, farm equipment, consumer appliances, steel, automobiles, and aerospace. In this broader context, they add at least $100 billion a year to our economy.

Machine tools also play an important part in ensuring our military security. In times of war, we must be able to manufacture military equipment and hardware as quickly as possible. The key to accomplishing this lies in a strong machine tool industry. One that was inefficient and out of date could seriously damage our military readiness and strength.

As recently as the 1960s, U.S. manufacturers were the preeminent makers of machine tools in the world. In 1965, American-made products accounted for more than 30 percent of the world market and 20 percent of world exports. By 1980, however, the Germans had supplanted us as the international leader. Our total market share had declined to only half of what it had been fifteen years before and our share of world exports had decreased by 70 percent.

We are now in danger of losing our home market. Between 1970 and 1980, imports of foreign-made machine tools increased tenfold, and they now account for 25 percent of all machine tools sold here. In 1970 our exports were twice our imports. By the end of the 1970s, we were running a trade deficit of $500 million. In addition to individual deficits with Japan, West Germany, and France, we even managed to fall into red ink with Italy, Great Britain, Switzerland, Sweden, and Taiwan.

The future looks no better. Japan, West Germany, and other Western European nations are preparing an even stronger assault, for they see a booming American market in the coming years and want to be sure to benefit from it. Detroit is in the process of downsizing its entire line of automobiles, and will need completely new manufacturing equipment. The surging aerospace industry also promises to be a lucrative market. Foreign competitors are determined to capitalize on these opportunities.

At least fifteen foreign machine tool manufacturers have built production and assembly plants in the United States. In addition, foreign competitors are buying into our market and our technology by purchasing American companies. In 1979, the Swiss firm of Derlikon-Buhrle Holding bought Motch & Merryweather Machinery Company, the largest distributor of machine tools in the United States. A year later Thyssen, the West German steel giant, bought Place Machine Sales Corporation, a medium-sized firm with sales of over $30 million in 1980. Many other foreign machine tool manufacturers are reportedly studying the possibility of opening their own plants here or acquiring existing American firms.

Are American manufacturers prepared to face this new competition? According to a U.S. Army study, the answer is no. The study concluded that American machine tool manufacturers are losing the technological edge they once enjoyed in both design and manufacturing. Evidence of this trend is visible in the patent area. In the early 1960s, American firms received nearly 84 percent of world patents on metalworking machinery, but by 1980 this had declined to about 50 percent.

The major reason for this, according to the Army, is that severe price competition has led American companies to abandon a full commitment to research and development. The report characterizes the R&D programs of most machine tool manufacturers as "low level" and "erratic." A survey of firms in the industry revealed that expenditures on R&D as a percentage of sales was only 1.5 percent. Foreign companies spend three or four times as much.

The same short-sighted management that has failed to invest in R&D has also failed to build necessary capacity. In 1980, American manufacturers held a backlog of orders totaling more than $5 billion, or the equivalent of an entire year's output. The delivery time for some specialized equipment was running as long as three years. Because of this backlog, potential customers have turned to foreign manufacturers that are able to supply the needed equipment more quickly. The Army report emphasized that foreign machine tool manufacturers are not only superior to their American counterparts in technology, quality, and price, but are also far more prompt in delivery.

A further problem created by management's short-sightedness is the lack of skilled workers in the industry. Because of cyclical demand, work forces have been drastically cut when orders fell and expanded when demand revived. More than 120,000 machine tool workers in 1967 declined to a low of 80,000 in 1972 before rebounding to 100,000 in 1980. This hiring and firing undermined job security and caused many skilled workers to leave the industry permanently. Consequently, as the industry attempts to prepare itself for the expected boom market of the 1980s, the largest bottleneck is the lack of skilled workers. There is already a 25 percent shortfall of qualified labor and this problem could become worse.

Yet another handicap the industry faces is declining productivity. Over the ten-year period between 1967 and 1977, productivity actually fell an average of one percent a year. A major reason for this extraordinary phenomenon is that machine tool manufacturers have continued to use old and inefficient plant and equipment in making their products. A recent survey found that plant and equipment used by machine tool makers was much older than that of other manufacturing industries in the United States.

The Army report speculates that the industry's poor investment record may have resulted in part from a recent avalanche of rules and regulations pertaining to worker safety and pollution control. Manufacturers complain that they have had to divert funds to meet regulations—funds that would otherwise have been invested in new plant and equipment.

The American machine tool industry suffers from a serious structural problem as well: it is made up of a large number of small firms. A majority of the 1200 firms in the industry reported sales of less than $5 million a year in 1980, and more than 1000 employ fewer than 100 persons. Even the largest firms in the industry are relatively small. According to *American Machinist*, the five leading firms in 1980 were:

| | *1980 Sales* |
Company	*(in millions)*
Cincinnati Milacron	$563
Bendix Industrial Group	$475
Cross & Trecker	$320
Ex-Cell-O	$290
Acme Cleveland Corp.	$257

A logical course of action would be for smaller companies to merge in order to consolidate their R&D efforts and to gain economies of scale. That is exactly what Cross Company and Kearney & Trecker Corporation had in mind when they announced a proposed merger in 1979. According to spokesman for the two firms, "the merger was agreed to in order to create a technologically sound company with the resources to become a strong competitor in the world marketplace."

The Justice Department had other ideas, however, and filed an antitrust suit against the two firms to prevent their merger on the grounds that it might preclude future competition in the industry. The suit was dropped in 1981 and the merger completed, but for two years the companies were left in limbo, and other companies were doubtless discouraged from mergers by the threat of government opposition.

While business and government fight each other in the United States, our competitors abroad are strongly supported by their governments. West German companies, exporters of over $200 million worth of machine tools to the United States in 1980, receive government support in research and development. A consortium of four of the country's leading universities has established specialized machine tool research and development centers on their campuses. These laboratories receive 50 percent of their funds from the government. Japanese manufacturers, who shipped approximately $500 million worth of machine tools to the United States in 1980, receive the usual strong backing of "Japan, Inc."

Governments of the newly industrializing countries are also trying to develop machine tool industries. In 1980, Taiwan shipped more than $100 million worth of machine tools to the United States, and South Korea is not far behind with a product line of basic machine tools for drilling, boring, and sawing. With government help, it should not be long before South Korean companies become major competitors in the world market.

Our machine tool industry is clearly in danger of falling into foreign hands. Its defenses are weak. To lose this important industry to our competitors would be a serious blow to both our economic and military well-being.

Part Seven

Counterattack

The American problem is not returning to some golden age of economic growth (there was no such golden age) but in recognizing that we have an economic structure that has never in its history performed as well as Japan and West Germany have performed since World War II. To retreat into our mythical past is to guarantee that our days of economic glory are over.

—LESTER C. THUROW,
The Zero-Sum Society

35 Closing the Borders

After World War Two, the United States nurtured an emerging world economy by helping to remove international trade barriers. Yet others, not this country, primarily benefited.

Under these circumstances it is not unreasonable to ask whether we should demand a change in the rules or even leave the game entirely. Why not simply shut down the borders of our enormous market and continue in a state of happy and self-sufficient isolation?

There have always been strong voices in favor of such a policy. Polls by *The Wall Street Journal* and the Roper organization indicate that the public supports protectionism over free trade by a margin of nearly two to one. The late George Meany, leader of the AFL-CIO labor federation for most of the postwar period, used to describe free trade as "a joke and a myth." Former Representative Charles Vanik (D-Ohio), former chairman of the House Subcommittee on Trade, argued throughout the late 1970s for an automatic import surcharge to be placed on foreign goods whenever the United States trade deficit reached a critical level. In 1978, Edward Bernstein, eminent Washington economist and consultant, friend of Lord Keynes, and an architect of the Bretton Woods monetary system, which survived from the mid-1940s until the early 1970s, shocked the economic establishment by proposing a uniform American tariff of 10 percent on all imports.

Bernstein's reasons were presented to the press in his usually trenchant style: "If you take the world's [1977] trade deficit with OPEC you'll see that about three-fourths of it is accounted for by the United States deficit. So you see, our trading partners are shifting their own deficits back on us. They see us as the leaders of the Free World, the lender of last resort, the employer of last resort, we're everything to them. They get scared, and run excessively cautious fiscal and monetary policies and count on maintaining their levels of employment and output by exporting to us, or some other region . . . I have told Congress that I have no objection to using our budget deficit to offset deficiencies in domestic demand. But I don't see why we should use our budget to offset unemployment in Japan and Germany and these other countries, which is exactly what we're doing when we let them swamp us with their goods."

Even the strongest proponents of free trade could not lightly dismiss Bernstein's argument. A uniform tariff, if set high enough, would reduce imports. It would protect new and promising industries, as well as old and fading ones. Perhaps most importantly, it would eliminate the present system in which Congress provides protection to whichever industries have the most political influence.

At the same time, conventional counterarguments for more—not less—free trade are also compelling. They can be reduced to five: inflation, productivity, jobs, stability, and global interdependence.

INFLATION

The linkage between consumer prices and free trade was summarized two hundred years ago by Adam Smith, the founder of modern economics: "In every country, it always is and must be the interest of a great body of the people to buy whatever they want of those who sell it cheapest. The proposition is so very manifest, that it seems ridiculous to take any pains to prove it; nor could it have been called into question, had not the self-interested sophistry of merchants and manufacturers confounded the common sense of mankind."

Smith's point is well supported by recent events. Trigger prices used to subsidize the steel industry cost American consumers $1 billion a year. Import restrictions on beef, dairy products, and sugar cost an additional $1.5 billion. Conversely, Harbridge House, a leading business consulting firm, estimates that Americans saved over $8 billion on automobile purchases during the last decade because of the presence of foreign competition.

PRODUCTIVITY

Adam Smith's pupil, David Ricardo, demonstrated the importance of free trade for productivity and economic growth. By importing items that other nations produce cheaply, a nation's resources are freed for maximum productivity in areas of comparative advantage. Furthermore, as Joseph Schumpeter later added, productivity growth derives less from improvements within an industry than from the continual rollover of resources from older industries (such as autos and steel in the United States) to newer industries (such as semiconductors or biotechnology). If we close our doors to imports, capital that might otherwise shift to industries of the future would remain committed to industries of the past. The eventual result would most likely be economic stagnation.

JOBS

A common perception of protectionism is that it saves jobs. But for every job saved in a protected industry such as steel or automobiles, another job in a successful export industry may be lost. A study by Bank of America indicates that raising tariffs sufficiently to halve the 1977 United States trade deficit would have raised consumer prices by one percent without any net gain in jobs.

STABILITY

The present international economy has been built on expanding trade. If the United States abruptly raised its tariffs, other countries would undoubtedly follow. Marginal countries would then face bankruptcy; export-oriented companies might fail; and a worldwide depression could ensue.

The United States last embarked on a policy of radical protectionism during the Great Depression. The Smoot-Hawley Tariff Act of 1930 effectively closed the American market to a wide variety of foreign goods. Within a year, twenty-five nations retaliated with similar measures and worldwide economic conditions sharply deteriorated. Four years later, Congress had to reverse itself by passing the Reciprocal Trade Agreements Act.

GLOBAL INTERDEPENDENCE

The last argument in favor of free trade is that all nations—without exception—have become interdependent during the last few decades. The United States imports half its oil from abroad. We are also dependent on foreign suppliers for twenty key metals and minerals such as chromium, cobalt, manganese, and platinum, minerals crucial for military as well as industrial purposes.

Is protectionism then a valid alternative for the United States? Great Britain in the nineteenth century built the beginning of a world economy and vigorously defended free trade. If its leaders had foreseen the industrial decline and decay that subsequently unfolded, they might have adopted protectionism much sooner than they did. On balance, protectionism might have slowed and even softened the retreat that took place. But protectionism is at best a defensive strategy that merely postpones the consequences of defeat. The United States is not yet launched on an irreversible decline. There is still time to win the fruits of leadership in a genuinely international economy based, however precariously, on free trade. And while there is still time, the optimistic course is the only possible course for government and industry to adopt.

36 *"New Wisdom for a New Age"*
—JOHN MAYNARD KEYNES

Putting aside negative and defensive measures such as protectionism is a vital first step toward regaining mastery of world markets. It is not enough in itself, however. A second step—even more critical—is to learn to compete against increasingly powerful foreign adversaries.

Up to now, American companies have lacked neither resources nor opportunities. The missing ingredient has been an investment doctrine, a blueprint for deploying the powerful forces at our disposal. In effect, we have needed a set of concepts to help us manage the capital and human assets that all too often have been squandered in the past.

In searching for such a doctrine, we need not look to Japan. The most useful elements of modern business theory were developed in the United States—in some cases as long ago as the early 1960s. Taken together, these elements attempt to answer the most fundamental question facing American industry: how to orchestrate prices, costs, investments, products, and markets in a coherent and successful international business strategy.

CONCEPT ONE:
INTERNATIONAL GRAND STRATEGY

At the simplest level, the purpose of business strategy is to gain a fundamental advantage over competitors. This can be accomplished in only one of two ways: create a more desirable product or make the same product for less. These basic alternatives can in turn be expanded into four:

Product Advantage	*Cost Advantage*
New or significantly improved product	Reduce labor costs through automation, mass production
More reliable version of old product	Substitute cheaper labor

What is most notable about Japanese and other effective competitors is the clarity of their overall business strategies. In steel, the Japanese first sought to exploit their low wage rates. When their labor costs increased, they turned to automation and mass production. In semiconductors, they relied on quality control and product reliability to create a beachhead. Once firmly established in the international market, they moved on to producing new and improved products. In computers, they are currently attacking the top of the market (the largest and most sophisticated machines) with innovative design and the bottom of the market (personal computers) with mass-production techniques.

These strategies are effective because they exploit American weaknesses. In some instances, they also expose an American inability or unwillingness to fight back. Faced with a quality-control strategy in semiconductors, American manufacturers should have responded with a counterstrategy of their own. Matched dollar for dollar on this kind of expenditure, the Japanese might have been denied any advantage from their investment. In time, they might have retrenched or even abandoned the game.

More importantly, American semiconductor companies should have carried the struggle to the competitors' home ground by undertaking an export campaign with aggressive price cutting in Japan and elsewhere in the Far East. Even with domestic demand for semiconductors far outstripping domestic supply, some part of American manufacturing capacity should have been channeled overseas to harry the Japanese offensive at its source. With their own and adjacent markets secure, Japanese producers had both time and opportunity on their side.

CONCEPT TWO: GLOBAL MARKET SHARE

Market share theory is the most important innovation in economics since the Keynesian Revolution of the 1930s and 1940s. It states in essence that the highest-volume producer in a properly defined business enjoys measurably lower costs and higher profitability than other competitors.

The Boston Consulting Group is usually credited with developing market share theory in its present form. Beginning in the late 1960s, the firm demonstrated that the cost of producing and distributing a wide variety of goods including beer, aluminum, integrated circuits, and low-density polyethylene declined in real (inflation adjusted) terms by 20 or 30 percent with each doubling of output. The conclusion to be drawn from these studies was that economies of scale and so-called learning curves (the tendency of workers to become more skillful and productive with experience) were much more valuable than anyone previously had thought.

The Marketing Science Institute of the Harvard Business School (now independently incorporated as the Strategic Planning Institute) was able to confirm the Boston Consulting Group's hypothesis. The institute surveyed hundreds of major American companies on a confidential basis. Results indicated that a 10 percent advantage in market share was accompanied by an average improvement of about 5 percent in pretax return on investment. Businesses with shares in excess of 37 percent earned an average return on investment three times greater than those with shares of 7 percent or less. The effect was so strong that even high-share businesses (those with over 26 percent of the market) that described their product as one of inferior quality earned a higher return than better-quality but lower-share competitors.

American businessmen were slow to accept these findings. The traditional view was expressed by a *Harvard Business Review* article of the 1960s: "Targets stated in terms of market share may be in conflict with other goals of the firm, such as maximum short-run or long-run profits. . . . Management must . . . recognize the danger of a conflict between market share and other more valid objectives."

Not surprisingly, American executives complained that Japanese and other foreign companies were irrational in their pursuit of international sales at the expense of short-term profitability. In fact, Japanese companies were anything but irrational. Whatever near-term strategy they adopted—innovation, quality, or aggressive pricing—their ultimate goal was always global market share. When they appeared to be dumping their products at exceptionally low prices, they were usually doing so to gain additional volume and thus further reduce their operating costs. In the end, Japanese competitors dominated major global markets and earned handsome profits even at modest prices.

Not all American executives failed to grasp the game that was being played. Some understood it very well. But understanding market share theory was not sufficient; it had to be implemented properly. Some managers refused to define their markets in international terms.* Only a small number of American firms bother to export. One percent of all U.S. firms account for 85 percent of all our exports. According to former Assistant Secretary of Commerce Frank A. Weil, at least 20,000 more U.S. companies could be selling goods in foreign markets than are currently doing so. By underemphasizing exports, especially to the Far East, U.S. manufacturers abdicated the struggle for global sales volume.

Other mistakes were made as well. American companies often established separate subsidiaries and plants in each major foreign market rather than concentrating production in one place. As a result, potential economies of scale and learning curves were needlessly sacrificed. In some instances, executives acted as if unit cost savings would automatically flow from market share gains. New cost reductive technologies such as CAD/CAM and robotics were endlessly studied but only rarely put to full use. The automobile industry in particular remained much more labor intensive than its scale warranted.

CONCEPT THREE:
INDUSTRY LIFE CYCLE

Businessmen have always thought about industry growth in human terms such as infancy, adolescence, maturity,

*Defining relevant market shares is an admittedly complex task. On one level, it involves geography: regional versus national versus international markets. On another level, it involves product or customer distinctions. Depending on the context, it may be desirable to focus on a computer market, a mainframe computer market, or a mainframe scientific computer market. On a third level, share definition depends on manufacturing and marketing cost structure. Two very different products may be manufactured in the same facility using common equipment. Consequently, their automation and mass-production potential must be analyzed together. Such complications are currently the subject of heated debate among business school professors and consultants. However, they are quite secondary to the central implications of market share theory.

decline, and death. Some industries, such as high-fashion apparel, race through all five stages in a few years or even months. Others, such as industrial bolts, require several generations. Sometimes the process is unpredictable. Nylon, developed for military use, was reborn for consumers. Some industries with a long expected life die instantly.

Until recently, business managers could not explain such phenomena. With the appearance of market share theory, however, the pieces fell into place. Although the length of a life cycle depends on many variables, it depends above all on pricing. If an innovator launches a successful product but keeps prices high, other companies will enter the market. More and more competitors will earn less and less until demand is finally (usually quickly) exhausted. If, however, an innovator concentrates on market share instead of immediate profits, it accomplishes two desirable ends. First, as costs and prices decline with increasing volume, the number of potential customers able to afford the product increases, often dramatically. Second, lower prices discourage new competition.

Within the context of life cycle theory, American companies have made numerous mistakes. Characteristically, they have thought in terms of a shorter domestic cycle rather than a much more extended global one. They have also tended to overemphasize profitability early in the cycle when they should have been pricing aggressively and building share. When American television manufacturers were first confronted with Japanese inroads, they raised prices to protect profit margins. The result was a further decline in both market share and profits.

U.S. Steel offers a classic example of cycle misman-agement. The company allowed its domestic market share to fall steadily from 48 percent in 1910 to 34 percent in the mid-fifties to 23 percent in 1977. Consequently, none of the substantial profits that should have accompanied the aging of its domestic cycle were ever realized, By the time an international steel market appeared, the company's ability to compete was already fatally weakened. Yet as late as 1978, company executives were still pricing to maximize short-term profits. When the United States government established trigger prices for steel, thereby effectively increasing the cost of Japanese exports by 15 percent, U.S. Steel and other American producers promptly raised their prices by a like amount.

CONCEPT FOUR: INVESTMENT TIME HORIZON

American businessmen have always thought about profits in conventional accounting terms. One measure has been earnings per share of company stock. Another has been return on investment. The trouble with this approach is that a company can report accounting profits and still bankrupt itself, i.e., run out of cash.

The other problem with accounting conventions is that they are expressed on an annual basis. This is much too short a time in which to measure international market results. A major export drive may require ten years to succeed. In the early years, expenses will exceed revenues by a wide margin. Just adding necessary manufacturing capacity can require five years. It should be obvious that companies relying on an unsound measurement system will pursue distorted objectives. The process is circular, as misstated objectives lead to unwise investment decisions which lead eventually to failure in international markets.

The usual formulation of this syndrome is that American businesses are too profit-motivated. The reality is quite different: American businesses just measure their profits the wrong way. The right way is to use a technique known as "discounted cash flow." Although discounted cash flow has long been used by corporations to analyze investments in specific projects, most companies fail to use this approach in planning corporate strategy.

Putting aside the financial jargon and higher math, the basic concept of discounted cash flow is quite simple. First, managers must think in terms of cash rather than accounting conventions. Second, they must think in terms of cash over the entire life of a business, or at least over an extended period of time, such as ten years. They must calculate present worth of future cash flows after taking into account risk, inflation, and the time value of money.* Whatever specific formula is used,† the end result should be a different way of thinking and acting internationally. Freed from the short-term, but still closely tied to profit disciplines, American companies would finally be able to bring the full weight of their resources to bear on international markets.

CONCEPT FIVE: THE DIVIDEND TRAP

In an era of transition from domestic to international markets, the ability to invest represents raw industrial power. American companies, however, have been starved for capital. Debt has been steadily added throughout the postwar period until, in aggregate, debt capacity has been exhausted. Under these circumstances, one might assume that companies have reduced their tax burdens to the legal limit. Surprisingly, many have failed to do so.

---

*The time value of money theorem tells us that one dollar received today and invested at 10 percent is the equivalent of two dollars received in seven years.

†For a more detailed treatment of this subject, see Alfred Rappaport, "Selecting Strategies That Create Shareholder Value." *Harvard Business Review*, May–June, 1981, p. 139.

For example, many major companies still use accounting conventions that result in higher reported profits but also higher than necessary taxes.*

American companies also pay substantial dividends to their shareholders—money that could otherwise be used to build international market shares. In 1980, companies listed on the New York Stock Exchange paid out a total of $55.4 billion in dividends.

Admittedly, the practice of paying high dividends would be difficult to change. Tens of thousands of individual shareholders have bought stocks because of an implied promise of a dependable and growing stream of current income. Tax-free institutions such as pension funds have come to place special emphasis on dividend growth. Confronted by these pressures, some managements have even resorted to borrowing money to maintain payments to their own shareholders. Others have paid dividends from phantom accounting profits based on underdepreciation of plant and equipment. Even healthy companies have misallocated scarce capital by emphasizing their stock's yield at the expense of other considerations.

In part, the dividend question is one of financial rationality. Dividends, unlike interest payments, are taxed both at the corporate and the individual shareholder level. Once the dividend is in hand, a shareholder may have to pay up to two and one half times more tax than on a capital gain. Even firms without investment opportunities would theoretically be better off buying their own stock or that of other companies (dividends passed between two corporations are 85 percent tax free) rather than paying out dividends. Company shareholders who depend on regular investment income would fare at least as well by holding a combination of high-yielding bonds along with stocks.

---

*Especially FIFO (first in, first out) treatment of inventory.

Yet in the final analysis, it is not merely a question of either taxes or financial rationality. To compete in a global economy, American corporations must marshal their capital. Sometime in the distant future, it may be appropriate for dividends again to reach present levels. But for now, they are too high and represent a luxury we cannot afford.

CONCEPT SIX:
PREPARING FOR THE UNKNOWN

The great unknown for all advanced nations—the United States included—is the potential ability of developing nations to exploit cheap labor in basic industries. The United States, Japan, and Europe may be able to remain competitive in industries such as automobiles by making marginal product-design improvements and by automating production. On the other hand, even fully automated plants with little or no labor content may ultimately prove less economical than labor-intensive plants in Third World countries. It is a question that will not be fully answered for at least a generation.

If automation fails to save our basic industries, traditional strategies and assumptions will have to be reconsidered. International market share in particular may prove to be much less valuable than expected. American manufacturers in labor-intensive industries will be forced to move production offshore. The future of American industry will then depend overwhelmingly on our ability to innovate and build new businesses.

The process of asset redeployment would be wrenching. It would be rendered all the more difficult by intense competition with Japan and Europe for control of high-technology industries—those beyond immediate Third World competition. In such an environment, we would be reminded once again of the adage that countries do not become rich by running their businesses well. They become rich by choosing businesses of the future rather than businesses of the past. American companies must keep this steadily in view.

With the foregoing in mind, it is possible to formulate a few fundamental rules for competitive success in the new world-economy:

• Formulate a grand strategy involving a product or cost advantage for every business. Adopt explicit countermeasures against competitive strategies. Take the offensive in the home territory of a major competitor.

• No matter how large or small one's business, think in terms of international market share. Concentrate resources to make this feasible. Above all, manage volume gains to produce lower unit-cost gains.

• Temper business strategy to the industry life cycle. Invest aggressively for share early in the cycle when growth is still expanding the pie. Always think of life cycle in international terms.

• Set long-term as well as short-term objectives. Plan in terms of cash instead of accounting conventions such as earnings per share or annual return on investment.

• Hoard cash to finance heavy investments during the transition to a global economy. Review accounting practices and reduce or eliminate dividends wherever possible.

• Prepare contingency plans for a worst-case event such as a collapse of older American industries in the face of Third World competition.

These are the most basic rules of international competition. Some of them are virtual prerequisites for success. At the same time, familiarity with the game is not in itself enough. Each company must make the rules work in its favor. Company officers may spend a fraction—perhaps only a small fraction—of their time on corporate investment through acquisition/divestment, capital budgeting, expense budgeting, pricing, and financial policy. However limited, this is the time that counts. If the allocation of corporate resources proves fruitful, the war will be won. If allocation decisions are made as they have been in the past, either ad hoc or guided by misleading assumptions, the war will be lost. In either event, the quality of investment will tell.

Viewed in this light, corporate leadership is a relatively simple process. It does not require—indeed it suffers from—too large a staff, too much data, too much advanced mathematics, and too much emphasis on forecasting the future. The most skillful leaders recognize that the future is essentially unknowable.*

As Henry Kissinger has pointed out, a bureaucracy that demands the certainty of having all the facts will wait too long and find its options foreclosed. Boldness and risk-taking for its own sake will rarely prove rewarding for the long term. But risk-taking to capitalize on a carefully formulated investment plan is the essence of corporate statesmanship.

---

*One of the growth industries of the past fifteen years has been the development of so-called econometric computer models that purport to forecast the future of either a specific industry or an entire national economy. Careful analysis of results obtained to date suggest that corporate managers might just as well rely on astrology or the I Ching.

37 The Antitrust Illusion

The battle for industrial supremacy in world markets will be won or lost by, companies, not by governments. But at a time of close collaboration between most foreign companies and their governments, the stance of the United States government is odd, if not perverse. Many government officials continue to view private industry as a competitor rather than an ally. Although the attitude of the Reagan Administration is far different from that of the Carter Administration, the regulatory climate for business remains negative.

When most people are asked to cite instances of business regulation by government, they point to the Clean Air or Clean Water Acts or to legislation creating the Environmental Protection Agency, the Occupational Safety and Health Administration, or the Consumer Product Safety Commission. The heart of government regulation, however, lies in antitrust laws. Antitrust has so permeated the American psyche that it is simply taken for granted. Unfortunately, most antitrust regulation, unlike its counterpart in public health and safety, provides little or no benefit at an enormous cost. Founded on ill-conceived and outdated principles, it is a serious impediment to American economic success in the balance of this century.

The basic elements of antitrust date from the passage of the Sherman Act of 1890. Section One of the Act states that "every contract, combination in the form of a trust . . . or [other] attempt to monopolize . . . any part of . . . trade or commerce . . . , shall be deemed guilty of a misdeameanor." This act formed the basis of the landmark Supreme Court decision in 1911 to dissolve the Standard Oil Trust of John D. Rockefeller into a collection of smaller companies.

The Sherman Act was subsequently reinforced by the Clayton Act of 1914 which outlawed specific business practices (such as price discrimination against buyers) thought to restrain trade. Section Seven, as later amended, also banned corporate mergers that would significantly reduce competition or create a monopoly. The Clayton Act was further supplemented by the Federal Trade Commission Act of 1914. This statute both established the Federal Trade Commission and, in a key section as amended in 1938, held that "unfair methods of competition in commerce and unfair or deceptive acts or practices in commerce, are hereby declared illegal."

Subsequent amendments to antitrust law have included fines of up to $100,000 and prison sentences of up to three years for individual violators such as company executives and automatic treble-damage awards for those successfully suing corporations. The latter have made antitrust an especially fertile field for lawyers working on contingent fees.

Spurred by these laws, the Justice Department spent the 1970s and the early 1980s prosecuting major antitrust cases against IBM and AT&T. During the same period, the Federal Trade Commission was suing Kellogg, General Foods, and General Mills for allegedly monopolizing the breakfast cereal market. All three cases illustrate the vagaries of antitrust enforcement.

The Justice Department originally charged IBM with monopolization of the mainframe computer market in 1969, but found it impossible to prove that mainframes existed as a separate sphere from other computers or data processing equipment. After the case had dragged on for over a decade, testimony involving technology and market patterns had inevitably become dated.

The role of IBM in protecting American trade interests, and the potential strength of foreign, government-supported competitors was mentioned only by the defense and peremptorily dismissed by the prosecution. Significantly, every previous private antitrust suit launched against the company by competitors, a total of twenty-four, has been settled, dismissed, or won by IBM. By the time the government dropped the case in early 1982, IBM had spent millions in legal fees and countless executive hours. Even more importantly, the company's competitive strategies had been shaped for almost a decade by legal rather than economic considerations.

The AT&T suit, filed under the Ford Administration, was superficially similar. The government sought to break up the telecommunications giant into separate research, manufacturing, and operating companies. The case was nevertheless unique simply because of its scale. When the presiding judge ordered both sides to reduce the 1,872 pages of government charges, over 300 lawyers and aides squeezed together in twenty-nine document-filled rooms. By late 1981, the government and AT&T together had assembled and inspected a total of 20 million documents.

AT&T had been the subject of an earlier suit by the Justice Department in 1949. That suit was settled in 1956 by a formal consent decree between the company and the government in which AT&T agreed to limit itself to telephone and communications services. Western Electric, AT&T's manufacturing subsidiary, further agreed not to manufacture any equipment not actually used in the provision of these services. As a result, AT&T was unable to participate in the computer industry, even though computers were becoming increasingly linked to telecommunications. Foreign telecommunications companies were not similarly constrained. Germany's Siemens and Japan's Fujitsu developed systemwide communication networks centering on their own proprietary computer hardware.

By the terms of a fixed settlement reached in 1982, AT&T agreed to divest itself of affiliates responsible for local telephone services in exchange for the right to participate fully in all aspects of the computer, data processing, and telecommunications industries. It was a desirable resolution in that AT&T is now free to compete on a worldwide basis using the most up-to-date technologies. It is also a resolution that could have been achieved by legislative or other means without resort to the courts.

AT&T still faces a total of thirty-nine private antitrust actions. MCI (a provider of long-distance telephone services) and Litton Industries (a manufacturer of telecommunication equipment) have already won jury awards of $600 million and $92 million respectively. Under the treble-damage provisions, these awards will balloon to $1.8 billion and $570 million unless reversed or reduced on appeal.

The FTC suit in the dry-cereal market differed from the IBM and AT&T cases in that it was aimed at three companies rather than one. The general complaint was that the three companies accounted for 75 percent of industry sales and thus constituted a "shared monopoly." The specific charge was that the companies had tacitly agreed to compete through advertising and dealer promotions rather than through price. This had allegedly cost the consumer one-tenth of one cent per breakfast.

An odd feature of the FTC's case was that the specific complaint about pricing was inconsistent with the general charge about shared monopoly. If the three companies had competed aggressively on price, the result would undoubtedly have been an even more concentrated industry. Although the FTC complaint was finally dismissed in late 1981, it cost the three companies nine years of uncertainty and $25 million in legal costs.

Antitrust suits such as those filed against IBM, AT&T, and the cereal industry would be impractical remedies even if the underlying assumptions were correct. In fact, however, they are demonstrably false. The idea that smaller companies are more efficient and produce lower-cost products contradicts economies of scale and market share theory. As previously noted, large companies do not automatically produce cheaper products. American automobile manufacturers threw away many of their scale-related opportunities by failing to automate and by paying wages 50 percent higher than in other manufacturing industries. But large companies that are committed to market share enjoy innumerable opportunities to cut costs relative to smaller competitors in the same market.

Large producers in concentrated industries may indeed enjoy above average profitability. Such profitability need not, however, imply either higher prices or more restricted output than in a "free" market with hundreds of competitors. More often, it simply reflects lower unit costs. In any case, commodity industries most closely resembling the classical "free" market model, such as agriculture, are almost invariably subject to price interference and control by government. Although government intervention prevents concentration, it also eliminates the supposed informational and price competitive elements of a multifirm system. When government price-fixing is removed, as in the stock brokerage industry after 1973, the number of firms falls along with prices. Based on this experience, it is wrong to identify concentration as a cause of inflation. The reality seems to be the reverse: inflation takes the greatest toll on the least efficient producers in a market and thus increases concentration. Over time, concentration brings inflation under better control by enhancing productivity.

To defend industry concentration is not to attack small business. The optimal size of companies is a function of market size and industry life-cycle. Small companies traditionally supply a vastly disproportionate share of new technologies and jobs. They are the yeast of the system and their number has steadily grown throughout the postwar period. But as markets grow and age, the number of participants should fall and relative size increase. In the huge international auto market, even Ford Motors may be too small to achieve necessary economies. In the emerging international computer market, IBM may be just large enough.

Over forty years ago, the Austro-American economist Joseph Schumpeter argued that antitrust regulation was misguided. Today his disciples still constitute a minority. A leading "neoconservative" and theoretician of the Republican Party, Irving Kristol, has cautioned against extending deregulation into the antitrust realm. The head of the Antitrust Division of the Justice Department under President Reagan, William F. Baxter, has indicated that he will not make wholesale changes in enforcement guidelines. Even most critics of antitrust concentrate on marginal reforms. One proposal is to ban treble damages. Another is to revise or supplement the Webb-Pomerene Act of 1918 (which allowed firms to bid jointly on foreign contracts) to give American companies clearer antitrust immunity on foreign projects.

Of all the proposals that have appeared, the most important have been to establish innovation, economies of scale, and foreign competition as a priori defenses against monopoly charges and to permit companies to pool research and development efforts. These proposals have already been instituted to a degree despite a lack of supporting legislation. In the first instance, corporate defense attorneys persuaded federal courts that large companies should not be penalized for innovation, higher productivity, or efforts to defend themselves against strong foreign competitors. In the second instance, the Justice Department issued a 113-page booklet specifying the limited circumstances under which research pooling would be allowed. In both cases the reforms only created additional complexities: courts are as little qualified to evaluate innovation, productivity, and foreign competitors as businessmen are to evaluate 113 pages of regulations.

The best solution under these circumstances is not to reform but to eliminate root and branch. With the exception of price-fixing statutes, virtually all antitrust laws should be repealed. Both business and government would benefit from an end to chronic confusion and uncertainty. Billions of dollars currently spent to assess whether a particular price is too low (predatory) or too high (collusive) or whether a particular product defines an industry or is only part of an industry could be usefully redeployed. Most importantly, American companies would be freed for the first time to compete as vigorously as possible in world markets with all the intellectual and capital resources at their disposal.

38 USA, Inc.

For some years, there has been a curious debate in Washington. On one side are those who want the federal government to adopt an industrial and trade policy to support private industry in the battle for world markets. On the other are those who want the government to stand aside and "stop getting in the way of private industry."

It is a false, misleading, and even foolish debate. The United States, like any other developed or developing country, has always had policies to advance industry and trade. As early as the 1800s, government land grants were instrumental in creating canals and railroads. In this century, the Defense Department and NASA helped underwrite the emergence of our computer and micro-electronics industries.*

The problem today is not that private industry has too much or too little "assistance" from government, it is rather that the assistance is disconnected, ill-designed, and generally ineffective. No American administration in recent memory has committed substantial time, thought, or political muscle to the formulation and implementation of a coherent industrial and trade policy, and the present one is no exception. In his first eight months in office, President Reagan adopted industrial and trade initiatives that were wasteful at best and potentially harmful at worst. A few examples:

*As late as 1965, the federal government accounted for 70 percent of the market for monolithic integrated circuits, 60 percent of the market for power and special purpose tubes, and 40 percent of the market for connectors.

DEPRECIATION ALLOWANCES

In his 1981 tax act, the president greatly simplified the rules by which corporations deduct the cost of new capital and equipment on their income tax returns. He also sharply increased depreciation allowances and tax credits in order to encourage industry to invest more heavily. By 1986, when the new provisions are fully operative, the Treasury will lose about $60 billion in tax revenue. By 1990, corporations on average will have sufficient write-offs to pay little or no income tax. In effect, the new depreciation rules represent a gradual repeal of the corporate income tax.

Does this make sense? If the president had openly eliminated the corporate income tax, it would have been beneficial. All corporate taxes are ultimately paid by individual shareholders. By using corporations essentially as collection agents, we have depressed both corporate investment and total tax revenues over time. But repealing corporate taxes through the back door is another matter. By emphasizing depreciation allowances and tax credits instead of straight tax cuts, we are favoring older industries with large plant, equipment, and other physical investment needs, and penalizing newer industries with less plant and equipment.

Significantly, neither Germany nor Japan permit the across-the-board rapid depreciation authorized by the new tax act. The competitor with the most comparable write-offs is Great Britain. Yet Germany and Japan reinvest much more of their gross national product than the British.

The president's new depreciation rules may also have the inadvertent effect of stimulating mergers between new, fast-growing companies with high tax bills and older companies with lots of tax shelters. Although there is nothing inherently harmful in such a trend, it would represent yet another diversion of industry time and resources from more important pursuits.

AUTO QUOTAS

In spring of 1981, President Reagan imposed "voluntary" import quotas on Japanese automobiles for 1982 and 1983. The question is not necessarily whether automobile quotas are desirable; it is whether the president made the best use of a limited weapon.

The Japanese know that they must ration both tariffs and quotas in order to avoid retaliation from their trading partners. Their response is to protect infant and emerging industries rather than older and politically powerful ones. If we were to emulate them, we would be studying the desirability of protecting our robot manufacturing capability or perhaps even our more developed semiconductor industry. In the long run, building or maintaining strength in these "state-of-the-art" technologies is much more important than preserving several major American auto producers. We can deceive ourselves that such choices are not necessary—that we can have it all. But in reality, we have to choose. And on balance it is quite likely that the president made a mistake in adopting auto quotas.

SYNFUELS

The United States Synthetic Fuels Corporation was established by Congress in 1980 to assist private industry in the development of alternative fuel sources such as shale oil, coal liquefaction, coal gasification, and tar sands. The rationale behind the program was that the capital cost and risks of alternative fuel plants were beyond the capability of even the largest private energy companies. By sharing some of the risk through loans, subsidies, and loan guarantees, Congress hoped the corporation would accelerate the nation's progress toward energy independence. In this respect, synfuels is analogous to the federal government's canal, railroad, and roadbuilding programs of the past.

The Reagan Administration's attitude toward the corporation is still emerging. During the transition between administrations in late 1980 and early 1981, the current Synfuels chairman, Ed Noble, recommended that the corporation be dissolved. Since his appointment, he has notified Congress that he will proceed very cautiously in committing funds. If this is a case of making every dollar count, it is to be applauded. However, if the program is to be abandoned or crippled, the federal government will have abdicated its traditional and proper responsibility to foster the most capital-intensive innovations of the future.

EXPORT CREDITS

National governments in the West have traditionally supported "big ticket" export industries such as aerospace and nuclear construction in one of three ways. First, they have provided insurance against political hazards such as nationalization. Second, they have used foreign aid to stimulate exports. Third, they have offered cut-rate financing packages to prospective customers through special export financing agencies such as the Export-Import Bank of the United States.

Of these three subsidies, the last has become increasingly important in recent years because of spiraling international interest rates. The Japanese have been able to offer attractive financing because their own domestic interest rates have never reached American or European levels. But other exporters—particularly the French—have simply frozen export rates at low levels despite higher and higher domestic rates.

As of 1980, the French and others were spending $5 billion per year to ensure that their official rates were lower than anything offered by American companies. Faced with this challenge, the Carter Administration planned to increase our Ex-Im Bank's loan authorization to $5.5 billion in 1982—over five times the level of 1976. President Reagan, however, limited the Ex-Im's authorization to $4.7 billion in fiscal 1981 and $4 billion in fiscal 1982. Secretary of Commerce Malcolm Baldridge justified this action on political rather than economic grounds: "Politically, the Ex-Im cuts were necessary because voters and the Congress had to realize that everybody's ox had to be gored. The government has few aid programs for business. It's necessary for people to believe that we are cutting the budget across-the-board."

Proponents of more—not less—Ex-Im funding responded with several counterarguments. Labor unions noted that the bank had already funded $100 billion in American exports. Each $1 billion in exports is thought to translate into 40,000 jobs for American workers. Aerospace manufacturers emphasized that an initial sale of a new airplane to a particular customer almost guarantees subsequent sales over long periods of time. By holding back on financing at a crucial moment, Boeing's counterattack against Europe's Airbus Industries might be jeopardized.

Each of these arguments had some merit. They were not, however, the primary reason why President Reagan's export credit policy was ill-timed. As William Durka, a manager of General Electric's international trade, has stated the case: "The only way to put the financing of exports on a sound economic basis is to permit the Ex-Im Bank to compete so effectively that it convinces our foreign competitors they have nothing to gain by unsound financial practices. Then perhaps they'd return to the bargaining table in a mood more receptive to our proposals." Durka's point is well taken. The United States can no more afford to disarm unilaterally in the international trade arena than we can afford to disarm militarily. Export credits may eventually disappear—but only if it becomes apparent that no single nation can hope to benefit from them.

"CANADIANIZATION"

Export credits represent only one of numerous ways in which foreign governments seek to intervene in global markets and bend the rules in their own favor. Another case in point is the recent Canadian government plan to "Canadianize" energy and natural resource industries. In practice, this has meant forcing Americans to sell their shares in many Canadian companies—sometimes at firesale prices.

The Canadianization program was adopted as part of a larger industrial master plan. Its central premise—which may or may not be correct—is that low-wage competitors from the Third World will ultimately overwhelm most traditional Canadian industries. A "Japanese-style" counterstrategy of achieving preeminence in high technologies is deemed to be beyond Canada's reach, so the preferred alternative is to secure its place as a source of oil, gas, and other vital natural resources. The move against foreign ownership is not meant to be hostile or xenophobic—it merely follows the logic of the plan.

Despite this rationale, the Canadian program is unfair. It ignores the $10 billion Canadians have invested in open American markets and the recent increase in attempts by Canadian companies to acquire American assets. President Reagan should have reacted sharply against such an assault on the principles of cooperation and reciprocity that underlie the global economy. Instead, he chose to remain silent. In effect, the United States acquiesced in an act of international privateering. By doing so, we have aided and encouraged the forces of economic nationalism still rampant in the world.

AMERICA'S TRADE BUREAUCRACY

Trade issues in the United States government have traditionally been debated by at least a dozen different agencies. Players include the Commerce Department, the Treasury Department, the State Department, the Agriculture Department, the Office of the U.S. Trade Representative, the Ex-Im Bank, the Defense Department, and the White House. The system has been described by Senate Minority Leader Robert Byrd as one of "byzantine complexity."

President Carter further complicated the situation by moving commercial attachés in American embassies from State Department to Commerce Department jurisdiction. He also created a new commerce undersecretary for international trade with three assistant secretaries. Under the Carter plan, the special trade representative was supposed to be in charge of trade policy and the Commerce Department was to implement policy. To no one's surprise, the new division of responsibility proved just as confusing as the old makeshift arrangement.

When Ronald Reagan arrived in office, he put aside bipartisan congressional support for a unified cabinet-level department of industry and trade and left the Carter machinery in place. The consequences of this decision became apparent during the auto quota negotiations with the Japanese government. The Japanese were anxious to forestall congressional action against their imports and preferred to strike a deal with the executive branch. Their immediate problem lay in finding a spokesman for the new Administration. Among those vying for dominance on the automobile import issue were the secretary of state, the secretary of transportation, and the U.S. trade representative. Faced with total disorganization on the American side, the Japanese eventually stiffened their resistance and concluded a more favorable package than was originally expected.

RESEARCH AND DEVELOPMENT

In some instances, the president's initiatives have been disappointing for what they left out rather than what they included. A notable example is the lack of a specific incentive for industrial research and development in the Administration's tax legislation. With 78 percent of tax cuts aimed at individuals and 22 percent at spurring corporate investment in plant and equipment, the priorities seemed once again to be skewed toward the past rather than the future.

Japan by contrast provides an industry tax credit equal to 20 percent of any year-to-year increase in research and development expenditures. This is in addition to accelerated depreciation of R&D facilities and equipment, which can result in a 60 percent tax write-off in the first year alone.* Japan also encourages companies to pool research facilities and efforts. Above all, the Japanese government actively identifies and promotes specific technologies believed to be critical to the nation's future. In this area in particular, our government should learn from the Japanese.

FOREIGN TAX CREDITS

Foreign tax credits are supposed to compensate American businesses for taxes paid abroad. In theory, the system is simple: for every dollar paid in foreign tax (up to 47 percent of total income), one dollar is deducted from American taxes. In late 1980, however, the Treasury Department decided that many taxes paid to foreign governments were not taxes at all. Instead, they were royalty

*Importantly, Japan allows rapid depreciation or expensing of technology purchased abroad. American tax laws discriminate against imported technology.

payments and, as such, were not eligible for the foreign tax credit.

American companies operating abroad were stunned by this approach. For one thing, foreign governments often failed to make any distinction between taxes and royalty payments. For another, the Internal Revenue Service was unable to offer reliable guidelines or even to respond to requests for advance rulings. In effect businesses were left to their own devices. If they judged right, a foreign project might be profitable after-tax; if they were wrong, virtually all profits might be drained by taxes.

The Treasury Department under Secretary Regan has been sympathetic to business complaints about this problem but has failed to offer any specific relief. In the meantime, corporations must make five- and even ten-year capital commitments in a climate of uncertainty.

FOREIGN CORRUPT PRACTICES ACT

The FCPA was passed by Congress in 1977 to prevent bribery of foreign government purchasing agents and officials by American companies. Although the act served a useful purpose, its complex and difficult-to-interpret provisions made it an enforcement nightmare. Warren E. Kraemer, McDonnell Douglas corporate vice president for Europe, has described the situation: "Any person who has any association with us [must] certify, practically every time he answers the phone, that what he is doing is not immoral, illegal, or an attempt to influence or bribe someone with whom he is in contact. . . . Before we can pay an expense of an agent, which may be a taxicab ride, he has to have [his expense account] validated by an American consular authority."

Under these circumstances, the cost of accounting and compliance makes foreign business sometimes prohibitively expensive. Worst of all, American executives can never be entirely sure that they are operating within the law.

The Foreign Corrupt Practices Act is only one regulatory disincentive for American exports. Others are legislation prohibiting cooperation with the Arab boycott of Israel (also virtually impossible to define in legal terms), environmental and safety standards, and rules on military-related technology exports. The Reagan Administration is already on record as favoring relief in some of these areas. The U.S. trade representative has attacked legal "impediments" and "barriers" to trade by quoting the comic strip Pogo: "We have met the enemy and he is us." Yet despite this viewpoint, the Administration has generally avoided such emotionally charged issues in Congress. Time passes and American businessmen remain the most regulated exporters in the world.

The new Administration's first eight months illustrate much of what is wrong with our national management of industry and trade. In brief we have:

• Favored older industries by emphasizing the wrong kind of corporate tax cut;

• Used tariffs and quotas to protect older rather than emerging industries;

• Failed to provide strong government support for the most capital-intensive new technologies such as synthetic fuels;

• Failed to put sufficient financial muscle behind our opposition to export-credit subsidies of foreign governments;

• Failed to stand up against other forms of economic nationalism and attempts by foreign governments to take unfair advantage of the international market system;

• Failed to establish a single government agency in charge of industry and trade;

• Failed to provide strong tax incentives for industrial research and development;

• Failed to clarify poorly drafted laws or regulations covering foreign taxes, bribery of foreign officials, and other areas.

The federal government should take action in each of these areas. Even more importantly, it should consider its actions as a whole. Whatever specific measures are adopted, the larger task is to tie them together into an overall industrial and trade policy. So long as the government lacks such a policy, we will legislate, negotiate, and allocate dollars in a vacuum. Inevitably we will make more than our share of mistakes.

Virtually all of America's major competitors have long since developed rational policies with clearly delineated priorities in business regulation, corporate taxation, research and development, industrial development, and trade negotiations. The time has come for the United States government to do the same. The Japanese in particular have demonstrated that economic security in the new global framework is no less important than military security. If our government put as much time, thought, and effort into planning our economic defense as it puts into planning our military defense, our overall security would be immeasurably enhanced.

39 The Eleventh Hour

In 1966, Robert Heilbroner, noted economic historian and author, published a book entitled *Limits of American Capitalism*. In a memorable passage, he wrote that "there . . . [is] a wide consensus as to the most important challenges facing the nation in the future. . . . If the nation at large were to draw up a list of those matters that appeared of the greatest urgency for the future . . . we would find defense, economic stability and growth, foreign relations, poverty, civil rights, urban renewal, education, unemployment, mass transport, population control, and the like. . . . There would also be a striking common denominator to the problems on the list. All of them are problems in which the initiatory impulse, the financial support, the essential policy determinations, and the day-to-day guidance of programs would have to come largely from nonbusiness elites. To put it differently, the thing at which businessmen are best—the production and sale of marketable goods and services—is no longer the thing that stands at the head of America's list of needs."

Today, very few Americans still believe that business has ceased to play a central role in our national life or that issues such as defense, economic stability and growth, and urban renewal can be separated from the production of goods and services. This alone represents a major perceptual gain. At the same time, we are still suffering from other, potentially even more damaging illusions: that our economy is mature and cannot generate sustained growth and that in any case we can continue to produce goods and services as we have in the past, primarily for our own market, with only a secondary glance at the world around us. Taken together, these illusions are exceedingly dangerous. They provide a recipe for national decline and our eventual extinction as a leading industrial power. They entirely miss the point that we are not suffering what Keynes called the "rheumatics of age," but rather the birth pangs of a new era. The question is whether the United States will lead and participate in the new era as we have in the old.

In a recent address at Harvard University, Henry Rosovsky, dean of the faculty of arts and sciences and economic historian of Japan, spoke of the principal lessons to be drawn from Great Britain's fall from world power over the past century. In Rosovsky's view, these were three:

1. Between the start of the Industrial Revolution in the 18th century and today, approximately twenty countries have experienced modern economic growth. New countries are joining the parade all the time, and the early industrializers—primarily Britain, France, and the United States—are continually facing new challengers. At present the most rapidly growing area of the world is in northeast Asia, and it may be elsewhere in the future. The point is simple: remaining on top or in contention is not a static process.

2. It takes a long time to become aware of decline. Although most economic historians agree that Britain's climacteric [as the world's greatest industrial power] occurred about one hundred years ago, this fact did not really become a matter of public concern until after World War One. Forty years of relative decline may have been an insurmountable obstacle.

3. Although a great many reasons have been given for Britain's economic decline, in my opinion the principal factors were internal and human, and therefore avoidable: British entrepreneurship had become flabby; growth and industries and new technology were not pur-

sued with sufficient vigor; technical education and science were lagging; the government-business relationship was not one of mutual support.

Today the United States exhibits many of these same symptoms. Like Britain, we have allowed ourselves to be buffeted by change instead of seeking to exploit it. We have remained inward looking and ignored economic opportunities of epochal scale in the emergence of world markets. We have suffered a failure of nerve as well as understanding. Despite this, we have not yet caught the English disease—at least not in its terminal form. Forty years have not yet passed since the climacteric of our power. We may well be at the eleventh hour. But sufficient time remains to win the real world war, if only we have the will to do so.

Selected Sources

INTRODUCTION

Servan-Schreiber, J.-J. *The American Challenge.* New York: Atheneum, 1968.

1 THE AMERICAN COLLAPSE

Drucker, Peter F. "Japan Gets Ready for Tougher Times." *Fortune*, November 3, 1981, pp. 108–14.

Peterson, Peter G. "The Decline of the United States in the World Economy." New York: Lehman Brothers Kuhn Loeb, 1979.

_____. "Another View: The Reagan Consensus vs. The Reagan Program." Speech given before the Women's Economic Roundtable, March 18, 1981.

President's Report on U.S. Competitiveness. Washington, D.C.: U.S. Department of Labor, Bureau of Industrial Economics, 1980.

2 THE ALIBIS

Ball, Robert. "Getting Our Friends to Flex Their Muscles." *Fortune*, February 9, 1981, pp. 60–65.

Boston Consulting Group. Study for the U.S. Department of the Treasury on the U.S.–Japan market.

Peterson, Peter G. "The Decline of the United States in the World Economy." New York: Lehman Brothers Kuhn Loeb, 1979.

3 THE NEW INDUSTRIAL STATE REVISITED

Galbraith, John Kenneth. *The New Industrial State.* Boston: Houghton Mifflin, 1967.

Hays, Robert, and William J. Abernathy. "Managing Our Way to Economic Decline." *Harvard Business Review*, July–August 1980, pp. 67–77.

4 THE OECD REPORT

Facing the Future: Mastering the Probable and Managing the Unpredictable. Paris: Organization for Economic Cooperation and Development, 1979.

5 THE NEXT ROUND

Bowen, William. "Closing the Trade Gap Could Take Ten Years." *Fortune*, July 14, 1980, pp. 128–37.

Larson, Dale W. "The Macroeconomics of U.S. International Competitiveness." Paper presented to the U.S. Department of the Treasury. Washington, D.C.: Trade Policy Committee, Economic Trade Policy Analysis Subcommittee, June 25, 1980.

President's Report on U.S. Competitiveness. Washington, D.C.: U.S. Department of Labor, Bureau of Industrial Economics, 1980.

Schumpeter, Joseph A. *Business Cycles.* New York: McGraw-Hill, 1939.

———. *Capitalism, Socialism, and Democracy.* New York: Harper & Row, 1942.

7 ASSAULT ON SILICON VALLEY

Bylinsky, Gene. "The Japanese Chip Challenge." *Fortune*, March 23, 1981, pp. 115–22.

———. "The Second Computer Revolution." *Fortune*, February 11, 1980, pp. 230–34.

"Can Semiconductors Survive Big Business?" *Business Week*, December 3, 1979, pp. 66–86.

"The Chip Maker's Glamorous New Generation." *Business Week*, October 6, 1980, pp. 117–20.

"The Computer Industry IX." *Financial Times*, March 3, 1980.

"Japan's Chipmakers Start the March on Europe." *Economist*, January 26, 1980, p. 65.

"A Mainframe on Three Chips." *Business Week*, March 2, 1981, pp. 116–18.

"And Man Created the Chip." *Newsweek*, June 30, 1980, pp. 50–56.

"Microelectronics Survey." *Economist*, March 1, 1980, pp. 15–16.

A Report on the U.S. Semiconductor Industry. U.S. Department of Commerce, Industry and Trade Administration, Office of Producer Goods. Washington, D.C.: U.S. Government Printing Office, September 1979.

Rudnitsky, Howard. "Intel—Right Again?" *Forbes*, March 3, 1980, pp. 61–62.

"Shouldering in on the 64K Chip Race." *Business Week*, October 13, 1980, p. 56.

Sporck, Charles E. "U.S.–Japan Semiconductor Issues: The U.S. Point of View." Speech given at a joint conference of Semiconductor Industry Association and Electronic Industry Association of Japan. Palo Alto: National Semiconductor Corporation, November 14, 1978.

U.S. and Japanese Semiconductor Industries: A Final Comparison. Chase Financial Policy. Report prepared for the Semiconductor Industry Association, June 9, 1980.

Uttal, Bro. "The Animals of Silicon Valley." *Fortune*, January 12, 1981, pp. 92–96.

Wiegner, Kathleen K. "A Legend Comes Down to Earth." *Forbes*, March 30, 1981, pp. 32–33.

9 FLANK ATTACKS

"Fujitsu Ltd. Claims Technological Gains in Two New Computers." *Wall Street Journal*, June 1, 1981.

Givens, William, and William V. Rapp. "What It Takes to Meet the Japanese Challenge." *Fortune*, June 18, 1979, p. 106.

"Hitachi in the 80's: A Focus on Computers." *Business Week*, March 2, 1981, p. 38.

Hout, Thomas, and Ira C. Magazine. *Japanese Industrial Policy*. London: Political Studies Institute, 1980.

"Japan's Bid to Out-Design the U.S." *Business Week*, April 13, 1981, pp. 123–24.

"Japan's New Target: IBM." *Newsweek*, October 2, 1978, pp. 103–6.

Lehner, Urban C. "Japan Starting 10 Year Effort to Create Exotic Computer." *Wall Street Journal*, September 25, 1981, p. 29.

Marion, Larry. "Like a Dose of Medicine." *Forbes*, June 8, 1981, pp. 72–76.

1981 U.S. Industrial Outlook for 200 Industries with Projections for 1985. U.S. Department of Commerce, Bureau of Industrial Economics. Washington, D.C.: U.S. Government Printing Office, January 1981.

"Small Computer Shootout." *Time*, March 2, 1981, pp. 68–69.

Uttal, Bro. "The Coming Struggle in Personal Computers." *Fortune*, June 29, 1981, pp. 84–92.

———. "Exports Won't Come Easy for Japan's Computer Industry." *Fortune*, October 9, 1978, pp. 138–46.

———. "Japan's Big Push in Computers." *Fortune*, September 25, 1978, pp. 64–72.

11 VOICES IN THE SKY

"A Boost for a Rival to the U.S. Shuttle." *Business Week*, September 7, 1981, p. 46.

Bruno, Jim. "Electronic Mail: It Gets There Fast." *Administrative Management*, September 1979, pp. 28–29.

COMSAT Magazine. Washington, D.C.: Communications Satellite Corporation, 1980.

"Europe's Battle for the Sky." *Economist*, July 19, 1980, pp. 93–97.

"The Gold Mine in Satellite Services." *Business Week*, April 6, 1981, pp. 89–92.

"ITT: Groping for a New Strategy." *Business Week*, December 15, 1980, pp. 66–70.

Kaplan, Sheldon. "Moving Money with Today's Technology." *Administrative Management*, September 1979, pp. 30–32, 58.

Kleiner, Lydia. "Bird-Watching: The Future of Satellite-to-Home TV." *American Film*, pp. 30–31.

"A Market Where the U.S. Lags." *Business Week*, February 11, 1980, pp. 73, 76.

1981 U.S. Industrial Outlook for 200 Industries with Projections for 1985. U.S. Department of Commerce, Bureau of Industrial Economics. Washington, D.C.: U.S. Government Printing Office, January 1981.

"Northern Telecom's Dive into the U.S. Market." *Business Week*, October 17, 1977, pp. 144–46.

"Toward the 'Wired Society.' " *World Business Weekly*, June 8, 1981, pp. 29–37.

12 SCIENCE FICTION IN THE FACTORY

Bylinsky, Gene. "Those Smart Young Robots on the Production Line." *Fortune*, December 17, 1979, pp. 90–96.

Chakravarty, Subrata N. "Springtime for an Ugly Duckling." *Forbes*, April 27, 1981, pp. 58–62.

"Conservation on the Factory Floor." *Economist*, March 1, 1980, pp. 12–16.

"Fanuc Edges Closer to a Robot-Run Plant." *Business Week*, November 24, 1980, p. 56.

"Japanese Industrial Robot Production Soared 85% in 1980." *Japan Economic Journal*, p. 15.

"Robots Join the Labor Force." *Business Week*, June 9, 1980, pp. 62–76.

"The Robot Revolution." *Time*, December 8, 1980, pp. 72–83.

"The Speedup in Automation." *Business Week*, August 3, 1981, pp. 58–67.

13 CAD/CAM

Bylinsky, Gene. "A New Industrial Revolution Is on the Way." *Fortune*, October 5, 1981, pp. 106–13.

"CAD/CAM for the 80's." *Applicon Incorporated Annual Report*. Burlington, MA: 1981.

Donlan, Thomas G. "A CAD/CAM World? Maybe So, But Competition Is Mounting." *Barron's*, December 22, 1980, pp. 4–6, 20.

"The Factory of the Future Is Shaping Up on Computers." *Economist*, December 6, 1980, p. 95.

"From Concepts . . . To Realities." *Computervision Corporation Annual Report*. Bedford, MA: 1980.

"The Speedup in Automation." *Business Week*, August 3, 1981, pp. 58–67.

14 OFFICE OF THE FUTURE

"Can Canon Copy Its Camera Coup?" *Business Week*, January 28, 1980, pp. 41–42.

Chiba, Atsuko, and Kathleen K. Wiegner. "Different Story." *Forbes*, March 16, 1981, pp. 80–82.

"Competition Heats Up in Copiers." *Business Week*, November 5, 1979, p. 115.

"Exxon's Next Prey: IBM and Xerox." *Business Week*, April 28, 1980, pp. 92–103.

"Joining the Race to Sell the Office of the Future." *Business Week*, May 5, 1980, pp. 54–56.

Joseph, Raymond A. "Japan, Hoping to Duplicate Its Success in Auto Field, Battles Xerox for U.S. Sales." *Wall Street Journal*, January 15, 1981, p. 48.

"Olivetti Starts Its U.S. Turnaround." *Business Week*, January 12, 1981, pp. 38E–38F.

"Sony: A Diversification Plan Tuned to the People Factor." *Business Week*, February 9, 1981, pp. 88–90.

"Sony's Secretive Leap into Word Processing." *Business Week*, December 29, 1980, p. 48.

Uttal, Bro. "Xerox Zooms Toward the Office of the Future." *Fortune*, May 18, 1981, pp. 44–52.

"VW's Latest Model: The Office of the Future." *Business Week*, March 3, 1980, pp. 61–64.

Wiegner, Kathleen K. "Xerox, Here We Come." *Forbes*, March 31, 1980, pp. 117–20.

15 GENETIC ENGINEERING

"Biotechnology." *Business Week*, July 6, 1981, p. 56.

"Biotechnology: Research That Could Remake Industries." *Chemical Week*, October 8, 1980, pp. 23–30.

"Challenging the U.S. Lead in Biotechnology." *Business Week*, August 4, 1980, pp. 30–31.

"Chemicals and Textiles." *Japan Economic Journal*. November 4, 1980.

"A Fast But Bumpy Track for Biotechnology." *Economist*, April 5, 1980, pp. 73–74.

Impacts of Applied Genetics. Congress of the United States, Office of Technology Assessment. Washington, D.C.: U.S. Government Printing Office, April 1981.

"Industry Starts to Do Biology with Its Eyes Open." *Economist*, December 2, 1978, pp. 95–102.

"Shaping Life in the Lab." *Time*, March 9, 1981, pp. 50–59.

Wilkinson, James. "Engineering a Genetic Revolution." *New Scientist*, March 6, 1980, pp. 628–29.

16 ALTERNATIVES TO OPEC

Boffey, Philip. "An Earthly Furnace Fueled by Fusion Nears a Crucial Test." *Smithsonian*, March 1981.

Briggs, Jean A. "Shaping Up the Shipout." *Forbes*, February 16, 1981, p. 57.

_____. "Solar Power—For Real." *Forbes*, October 13, 1980, pp. 142–48.

Burck, Charles G. "Solar Comes Out of the Shadows." *Fortune*, September 24, 1979, pp. 67–75.

Curtis, Carol E. "Shaping Up Synfuels." *Forbes*, March 30, 1981, p. 36.

"Deals That Put a Lid on Rail Rates for Coal." *Business Week*, June 30, 1980, pp. 42–44.

Energy Information Administration. *Annual Report to Congress*, vol. 3. Washington, D.C.: U.S. Government Printing Office, 1980.

Energy Projections to the Year 2000. U.S. Department of Energy. Washington, D.C.: U.S. Government Printing Office, July 1981.

Glasstone, Samuel. *Fusion Energy*. U.S. Department of Energy. Washington, D.C.: U.S. Government Printing Office, 1980.

The National Energy Policy Plan. U.S. Department of Energy. Washington, D.C.: U.S. Government Printing Office, July 1981.

Seneker, Harold. "Clean, Plentiful Energy on the Way." *Forbes*, November 24, 1980, pp. 38–40.

Special Report on Energy. Washington, D.C.: National Geographic Society, February 1981.

Stobach, Robert, and Daniel Yergin. *Energy Future*. New York: Ballantine Books, 1980.

"What's Keeping Coal in the Ground." *Fortune*, August 25, 1980, p. 48.

17 AMERICAN INGENUITY

Boretsky, Michael. "Technology, Technology Transfers and National Security." U.S. Department of Commerce. Speech given at U.S. Army War College, Carlisle Barracks, PA, 1979.

Gilpin, Robert. "Technology, Economic Growth and International Competitiveness." Testimony presented to the Congress of the United States, Joint Economic Committee, Subcommittee on Economic Growth. Princeton: Princeton University, 1980.

Glasstone, Samuel. *Fusion Energy*. U.S. Department of Energy. Washington, D.C.: U.S. Government Printing Office, 1980.

"Innovation: Has America Lost Its Edge?" *Newsweek*, June 4, 1979, pp. 58–68.

"Innovation: Japan Races Ahead as U.S. Falters." *Science*, November 14, 1980, pp. 751–54.

Outlook for Science and Technology: The Next Five Years. National Science Foundation, National Research Council. San Francisco: W. H. Freeman, November 1981.

Ramo, Simon. "The International Contest for Technological Superiority." Speech given at the annual meeting of the American Association for the Advancement of Science. San Francisco: National Academy of Sciences, January 3, 1980.

Science Indicators 1978. National Science Board. Washington, D.C.: U.S. Government Printing Office, 1979.

Technology and Trade: Some Indicators of the State of U.S. Industrial Innovation. U.S. House of Representatives, Committee on Ways and Means, Subcommittee on Trade. 96th Congress, 2nd Session. Washington, D.C.: U.S. Government Printing Office, April 21, 1980.

"Vanishing Innovation." *Business Week*, July 3, 1978, pp. 46–77.

18 MOF AND MITI

"The Best of the Game—A Survey of Japanese Industry." *Economist*, July 18, 1981, pp. 1–29.

Drucker, Peter F. "Japan Gets Ready for Tougher Times." *Fortune*, November 3, 1980, pp. 108–14.

Givens, William, and William V. Rapp. "What It Takes to Meet the Japanese Challenge." *Fortune*, June 18, 1979, pp. 104–5.

Handbook of Economic Statistics. Central Intelligence Agency, National Foreign Assessment Center. Washington, D.C.: U.S. Government Printing Office, 1980.

"How Japan Competes." *Dun's Review*, July 1979, pp. 65–87.

"How Japan Does It." *Time*, March 30, 1981, pp. 54–60.

Japanese Industries. Tokyo: The Nikko Research Center, Ltd., October 1980.

"Japan's Economy Tomorrow." *Business Week*, January 30, 1978, p. 47.

"Japanese Multinationals Covering the World with Investments." *Business Week*, June 16, 1980, pp. 93–102.

Magazine, Ira C., and Thomas Hout. *Japanese Industrial Policy*. London: Policy Studies Institute, January 1980.

Monroe, Wilbur F. *Japanese Exports to the United States: Analysis of "Import Pull" and "Export Push" Factors*. Washington, D.C.: United States–Japan Trade Council, June 2, 1978.

"Must Japan Slow? A Survey." *Economist*, February 23, 1980, pp. 1–42.

Rose, Sanford. "The Secret of Japan's Export Prowess." *Fortune*, January 30, 1978, pp. 56–62.

The Vision of MITI Policies in the 1980's. Tokyo: Ministry of International Trade and Industry, April 10, 1980.

Vogel, Ezra. *Japan as Number One: Lessons for America*. Cambridge, MA: Harvard University Press, 1979.

19 THE EUROPEAN CHALLENGE

Carson-Parker, John. "France Flaunts New Economic Muscle." *Fortune*, May 4, 1981, pp. 256–70.

Current Foreign Exchange Information. New York: Price, Waterhouse & Company, January 1980.

Dornberg, John. "Can West Germany Work Another Miracle?" *Institutional Investor*, June 1981, pp. 257–68.

Dizard, John. "Export Credits: Is War Inevitable?" *Institutional Investor*, April 1981, pp. 231–47.

Dreyfack, Kenneth. "The Heavy Hand of Politics on French Industrial Policy." *Business Week*, January 26, 1981, p. 44.

The European Community's Budget. Brussels: Commission of the European Communities, 1979.

The European Community's Research Policy. Brussels: Commission of the European Communities, 1979.

Europe Information. Brussels: Commission of the European Communities, November 1980.

Farnsworth, Clyde H. "Gain Cited on French Trade Issue." *New York Times*, July 9, 1981, pp. D1, D19.

"France's New Look." *Time*, June 29, 1981, pp. 26–34.

Gall, Norman. "Has Germany Caught the American Disease?" *Forbes*, March 16, 1981, pp. 42–53.

Geddes, John M. "German Export Rise Eases Recession." *Wall Street Journal*, July 16, 1981.

German Industrial Policy. Boston: The Boston Consulting Group, 1980.

Germany. Paris: OECD Economic Surveys, June 1979.

"Germany: The Reluctant Ally." *Business Week*, March 3, 1980, pp. 66–73.

"Germany Versus Japan: Economic Confrontation." *Forbes*, November 24, 1980, p. 203.

"Germany: Why It Thrives." *Dun's Review*, December 1979, pp. 106–10.

"Good European." *Time*, September 30, 1946, pp. 29–30.

Handbook of Economic Statistics. Central Intelligence Agency, National Foreign Assessment Center, Washington, D.C.: U.S. Government Printing Office, 1980.

"Hesitant Recovery from a Sharp Recession." *Business Week*, February 2, 1981, pp. 37–53.

Holt, Donald D. "Getting Used to Mitterand." *Fortune*, June 15, 1981, pp. 111–15.

"How the Germans Keep on Winning." *The* [London] *Sunday Times*, January 20, 1980, p. 72.

Jinnin, David B. "The Miracle Economy Hits the Skids." *Fortune*, April 20, 1981, pp. 137–44.

Kessler, Felix. "France's Future: Mitterand's Course—Radical or Pragmatic—Still Seems Uncharted." *Wall Street Journal*, July 28, 1981, pp. 1, 14.

_____. "French Economy Faces Big Overhaul." *Wall Street Journal*, April 24, 1981.

Mauthner, Robert, Terry Dodsworth and David White. "France." *Financial Times*, June 16, 1980, Survey, pp. 1–8.

"Picking Winners with a Japanese Formula." *World Business Weekly*, February 23, 1981, pp. 7–8.

Servan-Schreiber, J.-J. *The American Challenge.* New York: Atheneum, 1968.

Steps to European Unity. Federal Republic of Germany: Commission of the European Communities, 1981.

"West Germany 1981—Challenge and Change." *Wall Street Journal*, July 10, 1981, pp. 20–24.

20 NICs

Heenan, David H., and Warren Keegan. "The Rise of Third World Multinationals." *Harvard Business Review*, January–February 1979, p. 105.

International Financial Statistics. International Monetary Fund. January 1979.

Report to the President on Prices and Costs in the United States Steel Industry. Council on Wage and Price Stability. October 1977.

Steel: Background Data on the American Steel Industry and International Steel Trade. Report of the Subcommittee on Trade of the Committee on Ways and Means, 96th Congress, 2nd Session, U.S. House of Representatives, May 16, 1978.

The United States Steel Industry and Its International Rivals: Trends and Factors Determining International Competitiveness. Federal Trade Commission, Bureau of Economics. November 1977.

World Steel Trade: Current Trends and Structural Problems. Hearing before the Subcommittee on Trade of the Committee on Ways and Means, 95th Congress, 1st Session, U.S. House of Representatives, September 20, 1977.

21 THE CHINA FACTOR

Briggs, Jean A. "The Inscrutable West." *Forbes*, June 23, 1980, p. 39.

Chapman, William, "Two Asian Giants Enter New Era of Prosperous Friendship." *Washington Post*, October 22, 1978, p. A10.

"China: Bureaucratic Failures Are Stifling High Growth." *Business Week*, April 27, 1981, pp. 70–74.

"China: Indecision and Taiwan May Delay Oil Plans." *Business Week*, February 16, 1981, p. 37.

"China: Rescinding Reforms in the Face of Inflation." *Business Week*, April 6, 1981, p. 44.

"China: The Start of a $350 Billion Long March." *Business Week*, November 6, 1978, pp. 76–78.

Ching, Fran. "Problems Building Steel Mill Reflect Failure of China's Modernization Drive." *Wall Street Journal*, September 2, 1981, p. 40.

Facing the Future: Mastering the Probable and Managing the Unpredictable. Paris: Organization for Economic Cooperation and Development, 1979.

Lieberthal, Kenneth. "A Second Revolution Begins in China." *Fortune*, October 23, 1978, pp. 94–108.

"The New Threat to China's Economy: Inflation." *Business Week*, January 19, 1981, pp. 38–48.

Rowen, Hobart. "China's Oil: Peking Turns to West for Its Technology." *Washington Post*, August 11, 1978, pp. A1, A8.

22 THE "SICK MAN" OF THE EAST

Ball, Robert. "Europe Warms to Soviet Gas." *Fortune*, June 1, 1981, pp. 76–80.

Flint, Jerry. "Welcome to the Club." *Forbes*, October 13, 1980, pp. 61–64.

Handbook of Economic Statistics. Central Intelligence Agency, National Foreign Assessment Center. Washington, D.C.: U.S. Government Printing Office, 1980.

"Losing Ideological Steam." *Forbes*, May 28, 1979, p. 107.

Melloan, George. "Soviet Productivity Unwinds." *Wall Street Journal*, July 10, 1981.

Meyer, Herbert E. "The Coming Soviet Ethnic Crisis." *Fortune*, August 14, 1978, pp. 156–66.

Moynihan, Daniel Patrick. "Will Russia Blow Up?" *Newsweek*, November 19, 1979, pp. 144–47.

"Russian Robots Run to Catch Up." *Business Week*, August 17, 1981, p. 120.

"Soviet Imperialism Is in the Red." *Fortune*, July 13, 1981, pp. 107–8.

"Soviet Union: Deep Rooted Problems Force a Showdown." *Business Week*, April 27, 1981, pp. 69–70.

23 THE AMERICAN BREADBASKET

Agricultural–Food Policy Review: Perspectives for the 1980's. U. S. Department of Agriculture. Washington, D.C.: U.S. Government Printing Office, 1981.

"The Frost That Saved Brazil's Orange Trade." *Business Week*, February 9, 1981, pp. 25–27.

Hamilton, Martha M. "Shortage of U.S. Farmland Predicted." *Washington Post*, January 17, 1981, p. B1.

The Issues. Washington, D.C.: American Soybean Association, 1981.

"Major U.S. Soybean Competitors." *Foreign Agriculture*, August 21, 1978.

1978 Statistical Yearbook. New York: United Nations, 1979.

"Our Butter-and-Egg Men." *Fortune*, May 19, 1980, pp. 146–54.

"Perspectives for the 1980's." *Agricultural–Food Policy Review*, 1980, p. 15.

Report to the President on U.S. Competitiveness. U.S. Department of Labor, Office of Foreign Economic Research, Washington, D.C.: U.S. Government Printing Office, 1981.

Sinclair, Ward. "America's Farmland Is Washing Away." *Washington Post*, July 25, 1981, p. A11.

Social Aspects of Brazilian Economic Development. London: Brazilian Embassy, December 1974.

Tamarkin, Bob. "The Growth Industry." *Forbes*, March 2, 1981, pp. 90–94.

"The Technocrats." *Economist*, January 5, 1980, pp. 3–14.

Vollrath, Thomas. "An Examination of Factors Influencing the Competitive Position of Principal Exporters of Wheat, Corn and Soybeans." Unpublished paper. October 1979, pp. 4, 9, 14.

24 CHEMICAL WARFARE

"ASEAN on Road to CPI Growth." *Chemical Week*, March 19, 1980, pp. 32–38.

"Crime Pays." *Forbes*, September 29, 1980, p. 61.

Curtis, Carol E. "Rx: Made in Japan." *Forbes*, August 17, 1981, p. 37.

Facing the Future: Mastering the Probable and Managing the Unpredictable. Paris: Organization for Economic Cooperation and Development, 1979.

"Facts & Figures." *Chemical & Engineering*, June 8, 1981, pp. 30–83.

"French Chemical Producers See a Big Future Abroad." *Chemical Week*, October 1, 1980, pp. 35–38.

Gibson, Paul. "How the Germans Dominate the World Chemical Industry." *Forbes*, October 13, 1980, pp. 155–64.

"Japan's Drug Makers Try World Market, Challenging U.S. and Europe Producers." *Wall Street Journal*, August 7, 1981, p. 36.

The Kline Guide to the Chemical Industry.

Kosman, William C. "U.S. CPI Set for New Global Challenges in the 1980's." *Chemical Week*, May 21, 1980, pp. 34–42.

1981 U.S. Industrial Outlook for 200 Industries with Projections for 1985. U.S. Department of Commerce, Bureau of Industrial Economics. Washington, D.C.: U.S. Government Printing Office, January 1981.

"Super Glues Get Two New U.S. Producers." *Chemical Week*, August 6, 1980, p. 59.

26 THE UNFRIENDLY SKIES

"Aerospace: Buy European." *Newsweek*, April 17, 1978, p. 83.

"Aérospatiale's Raids on U.S. Helicopters." *Business Week*, December 22, 1980, pp. 34–35.

Ball, Robert. "Who's That Chasing After Boeing?" *Fortune*, April 21, 1980.

"A Challenge to the U.S. in Aerospace." *Business Week*, June 5, 1978, p. 64.

"Foreigners Corner a Hot Market." *Business Week*, October 13, 1980, pp. 162–65.

"Germany: Carving Out a Major Role in Aircraft." *Business Week*, May 1, 1978, p. 44.

Hanley, John. "The Day Innovation Died." *Vital Speeches of the Day*, November 1, 1978, p. 56.

Kraar, Louis. "Boeing Takes a Bold Plunge to Keep Flying High." *Fortune*, September 25, 1978, pp. 43–50.

"Masters of the Air." *Time*, April 7, 1980, pp. 37–46.

Menzies, Hugh. "U.S. Companies in Unequal Combat." *Fortune*, April 9, 1979, pp. 104–5.

Minard, Lawrence. "Vive l'Helicoptère!" *Forbes*, April 16, 1979, p. 75.

1980 Annual Report of the Commuter Airline Industry. Washington, D.C.: Commuter Airline Association of America, 1980.

1981 U.S. Industrial Outlook for 200 Industries with Projections for 1985. U.S. Department of Commerce, Bureau of Industrial Economics. Washington, D.C.: U.S. Government Printing Office, January 1981.

Nulty, Peter. "Friendly Skies for Little Airlines." *Fortune*, February 9, 1981, pp. 45–52.

"Reader's Report." *Business Week*, October 23, 1978, p. 11.

27 "ENCIRCLE CATERPILLAR"

"The 50 Leading Exporters." *Fortune*, September 22, 1980, pp. 111–12.

"The Foreign Invasion in Heavy Machinery." *Business Week*, February 9, 1981, p. 21.

"IBH's Bid to Inch Up on Caterpillar." *Business Week*, April 20, 1981, p. 44.

Krisher, Bernard. "Komatsu on the Track of Cat." *Fortune*, April 20, 1981, pp. 164–83.

Lien, John A. "Construction Machinery: U.S. Industry Continues World Leadership but Dominance Declines." Paper. 566-7519. U.S. Department of Commerce, Bureau of Industrial Economics. August 19, 1981.

1981 U.S. Industrial Outlook for 200 Industries with Projections for 1985. U.S. Department of Commerce, Bureau of

Industrial Economics. Washington, D.C.: U.S. Government Printing Office, January 1981.

29 THE LAST STAND

"The Battle Starts at Last." *Economist*, April 19, 1980, p. 70.

Color Television Receivers and Subassembling Thereof. Washington, D.C.: United States International Trade Commission, May 1980.

"Consumer Electronics." *Television Digest*, October 6, 1980, Vol. 20, No. 40, p. 15.

Consumer Electronics Annual Review. Washington, D.C.: Electronic Industries Association, 1981.

"Consumer Reports 1980 Buying Guide Ratings." *Consumer Reports*, March 1979, pp. 164–65.

Countertop Microwave Ovens from Japan. Washington, D.C.: United States International Trade Commission, February 1980.

"Japan's Chance to Sell Videodiscs in the U.S." *Business Week*, June 23, 1980, p. 33.

"Japanese Heat on the Watch Industry." *Business Week*, May 5, 1980, pp. 92–100.

"Japan's Strategy for U.S. Appliance Markets." *Business Week*, March 10, 1980, p. 82.

1981 U.S. Industrial Outlook for 200 Industries with Projections for 1985. U.S. Department of Commerce, Bureau of Industrial Economics. Washington, D.C.: U.S. Government Printing Office, January 1981.

"Philips—An Electronics Giant Rearms to Fight Japan." *Business Week*, March 30, 1981, pp. 86–100.

"Television Factbook." *TV Digest*. Washington, D.C.: Consumer Electronics Industry Association, 1980.

"TV: A Growth Industry." *Business Week*, February 23, 1981, pp. 88–102.

"The TV-set Competition That Won't Go Away." *Business Week*, May 8, 1978, pp. 86–88.

The U.S. Consumer Electronics Industry and Foreign Competition. Northwestern University Center for the Interdisci-

plinary Study of Science and Technology, U.S. Department of Commerce. Washington, D.C.: U.S. Government Printing Office, 1980.
"Videodiscs—A Three-Way Race for a Billion-Dollar Jackpot." *Business Week*, July 7, 1980, pp. 72–81.

31 TRIGGER PRICES

Annual Statistical Reports. American Iron and Steel Institute.
"Big Steel's Liquidation." *Business Week*, September 17, 1979, pp. 78–96.
Crandall, Robert W. "Competition and 'Dumping' in the U.S. Steel Market." *Challenge*, July–August 1978, pp. 13–20.
_____. "The Economics of the Current Steel Crisis in OECD Member Countries." Paper delivered to the Symposium on the Steel Industry in the 1980's. Paris: February 27, 1980.
"Is Europe 'Dumping' Steel?" *Newsweek*, March 31, 1980, p. 59.
"Labor Cools It with Big Steel." *Business Week*, April 28, 1980, pp. 26–27.
Lehner, Urban C. "Iron Will: South Korea Emerges as Steelmaking Power, Shaking World Market." *Wall Street Journal*, May 13, 1981, pp. 1, 24.
Sease, Douglas R., and Urban C. Lehner. "Steel Success: Japanese Steelmakers Thrive with the Aid of Government Body." *Wall Street Journal*, April 10, 1981, pp. 1, 26.
"Steel." *Forbes*, January 8, 1979, p. 108.
"Steel Talks: A Costly Pact, Even with Restraint." *Business Week*, February 18, 1980, pp. 122, 124.
"When Steel Wages Rise Faster Than Productivity." *Business Week*, April 21, 1980, pp. 144–48.

33 THE $165 BILLION QUESTION

"The Auto Clash Goes Global." *Dun's Review*, April 1978, pp. 49–53.

Ball, Robert. "Renault Takes Its Hit Show on the Road." *Fortune*, May 4, 1981, pp. 275–84.

_____. "Volkswagen Hops a Rabbit Back to Prosperity." *Fortune*, August 13, 1979, p. 120.

Bennett, Amanda. "GM's J-Cars Get Off to Slow Start, Victims of High Price, Short Supply." *Wall Street Journal*, July 23, 1981, p. 26.

_____. "Japan's Auto Makers Bolster Lines to Challenge Detroit's New Models." *Wall Street Journal*, October 14, 1980, p. 35.

Briefs, Godfrey E. "Can America Compete in the World Auto Market?" *Business Horizons*, December 1978, pp. 14–22.

Burck, Charles G. "A Comeback Decade for the American Car." *Fortune*, June 2, 1980, pp. 51–65.

Chapman, William. "Quota Drive Ended by Japan's Promise to Curb Auto Sales: Brock Endorses Plan by Tokyo on Car Sales." *Washington Post*, May 2, 1981, pp. A1, A14.

Cook, James. "A Tiger by the Tail." *Forbes*, April 13, 1981, pp. 119–28.

"Detroit Is Fighting Back." *Time*, May 11, 1981, pp. 56–57.

"Detroit's New Sales Pitch: Is It on the Right Road?" *Business Week*, September 22, 1980, pp. 78–88.

"European Motor Industry." *Financial Times Survey*, October 8, 1979.

"Ford's Financial Hurdle." *Business Week*, February 2, 1981, pp. 60–66.

"France: A Post-Election Rush to Buy into the U.S." *Business Week*, July 13, 1981, pp. 34–35.

Gall, Norman. "There Are No More Rabbits in Volkswagen's Hat." *Forbes*, August 17, 1981, pp. 71–75.

General Motors Annual Report 1978. Detroit: General Motors Corporation, 1979.

The Imported Automobile Industry: A New Assessment of Key Aspects of Its Impact on the U.S. Economy and the American Consumer. Boston: Harbridge House, June 1979.

"Japanese Exports Have Carmakers Quaking." *Business Week*, April 7, 1980, pp. 44–46.

Kanabayashi, Masayashi. "Japan Car Makers Eye Third World." *Wall Street Journal*, July 7, 1981, p. 33.

Koten, John. "Showroom Shock: Steep Price Increases for Detroit's '81 Autos May Dissuade Buyers." *Wall Street Journal*, October 3, 1980, pp. 1, 14.

Maus, Ervin III, and Richard L. Waddell. "U.S. Engineers Rank Imports Tops—In Quality, Not Technology." *Ward's Auto World*, March 1980, pp. 48–80.

"The 1981 Cars." *Consumer Reports*, Annual Auto Issue, April 1981.

"Peugeot and Chrysler: Ties That Hinder?" *Business Week*, June 15, 1981, p. 48.

Tamarkin, Bob. "The Latest Foreign Beachhead." *Forbes*, October 13, 1980, pp. 43–44.

"To a Global Car." *Business Week*, November 30, 1978, pp. 102–13.

Tucker, William. "The Wreck of the Auto Industry." *Harper's*, November 1980, pp. 45–60.

The U.S. Automobile Industry, 1980. U.S. Department of Transportation, Office of the Secretary of Transportation. Washington, D.C.: U.S. Government Printing Office, January 1981.

"U.S. Autos: Losing a Big Segment of the Market—Forever?" *Business Week*, March 24, 1980, pp. 78–88.

"The Wunderwagen." *Time*, July 20, 1981, p. 54.

34 THE TOOLS OF INDUSTRY

Economic Handbook of the Machine Tool Industry. McLean, VA: National Machine Tool Builders' Association, 1980–81.

"Foreign Competition Stirs U.S. Toolmakers." *Business Week*, September 1, 1980, pp. 68–70.

"Machine Tool Builders: Top Ten Builders." *American Machinist*, August 1981, pp. 59–61.

Machine Tool Industry Study—Final Report. U.S. Army Industrial Base Engineering Activity. Rock Island, IL: November 1, 1978.

1981 U.S. Industrial Outlook for 200 Industries with Projections for 1985. U.S. Department of Commerce, Bureau of Industrial Economics. Washington, D.C.: U.S. Government Printing Office, January 1981.

Technology of Machine Tools. Machine Tools Task Force, Lawrence Livermore National Laboratory, University of California, Vol. 1. Livermore, CA: October 1980.

35 CLOSING THE BORDERS

Bernstein, Edward. *Forbes*, August 7, 1978, p. 33.
Dun's Review, February 1978.
Minard, Lawrence. "Is Free Trade Dead?" *Forbes*, May 14, 1979, pp. 65–80.
Smith, Adam. *An Inquiry into the Nature and Causes of the Wealth of Nations.* (Glasgow edition of the works and correspondence of Adam Smith.) Oxford: Oxford University Press, 1980.
Thurow, Lester G. *The Zero-Sum Society.* New York: Basic Books, 1980.

36 NEW WISDOM FOR A NEW AGE

Perspectives on Experience. Boston: Boston Consulting Group, 1968.
Porter, Michael E. *Competitive Strategy.* Cambridge, MA: Harvard University Press, 1980.
Rappaport, Alfred. "Selecting Strategies That Create Shareholder Values." *Harvard Business Review*, May–June 1981, p. 139.

38 USA, INC.

Facing the Future: Mastering the Probable and Managing the Unpredictable. Paris: Organization for Economic Cooperation and Development, 1979.
"How to Regain Our Competitive Edge." *Fortune*, March 9, 1981, p. 82.
"Investment Incentives and Snake Oil." *Economist*, March 21, 1981, p. 76.
"The New Export Policy Works Like the Old—Badly." *Business Week*, July 21, 1980, pp. 88–94.

Reilly, Ann M. "Outgunned in the Export Credit War." *Dun's Review*, July 1981, p. 41.

39 THE ELEVENTH HOUR

Heilbroner, Robert L. *Limits of American Capitalism*. New York: Harper & Row, 1966.

Index

271